Rare Books Slavica
in the
University of Colorado
Libraries
Boulder, Colorado

Rare Books Slavica
in the
University of Colorado
Libraries
Boulder, Colorado

*An annotated
bibliography compiled
and edited by
Sonia L. Jacobs and Eugene E. Petriwsky*

ROBERTS RINEHART, INC. PUBLISHERS

BOULDER

International Standard Book Number: 0-911797-39-4

Library of Congress Catalog Card Number: 87-62074

Roberts Rinehart, Inc. Publishers
Post Office Box 3161
Boulder, Colorado 80303

Printed in the United States of America

CONTENTS

v

ILLUSTRATIONS

PREFACE

COLLECTING SLAVIC library materials on a limited basis at the University of Colorado Libraries originated in the 1930s. It was not until the 1960s, however, that organized acquisitions and processing of the materials began.

The Libraries do not have a special Slavic collection or division. The Slavic holdings number some ninety thousand volumes and periodicals, not including microforms, musical recordings, and tapes. The collection covers the humanities, social sciences, and some natural sciences and is intershelved throughout the system according to Library of Congress or Dewey classifications.

Rare Books Slavica at the Libraries originated with a handful of books and journals purchased mostly in the 1950s. Gifts and other purchases followed. At present, rare Slavica in the Special Collections Department comprises approximately two thousand items. The oldest Slavic title is Marquard Freher, *Rerum Bohemicarum antiqui scriptores aliquot insignes, partim hactenus incogniti . . . ,* Hanoviae, 1602 (No. 136). Some titles in the collection are autographed copies; many are first or limited editions. There are unusual printings, expensive facsimiles, rare maps, manuscripts, portfolios, and private correspondence.

This Rare Books Slavica catalogue covers materials published in Slavic languages or those related to Slavic studies regardless of language. Due to the diversity of language orthography, transliteration, and cataloging systems, it was not possible to adhere to an ideal format. Entries are in alphabetical order. Most transliterations of non-Roman alphabets are based on the simplified Library of Congress system. Alternative forms are cross referenced.

EUGENE E. PETRIWSKY

ACKNOWLEDGEMENTS

WE THANK Vice Chancellor Kay Howe of the University of Colorado and the Eugene M. Kayden Committee for awarding us a Kayden Grant. We thank University of Colorado President Gordon Gee for awarding us a grant from the President's Fund for the Humanities. Nora J. Quinlan, Head, Special Collections Department, and Professor Mark Wait of the College of Music encouraged us to persist in our endeavors. Professor Marvin Goodstein of the University of the South, Sewanee, Tennessee, provided valuable insight into the personal life of Eugene Kayden. Professors Nicholas Lee and Paul Babiak of this university provided endless hours of counsel, concern, and work on this joint effort. We especially thank J.K. Emery, friendly editor and fountain of advice. And, finally, we thank Lynn Lickteig, master photographer, Andrzej Wielgosz, artist and calligrapher, and Leonid Avrashov, our man Friday.

SONIA L. JACOBS and EUGENE E. PETRIWSKY

INTRODUCTION

HITHERTO UNKNOWN to most Slavic scholars, this collection of treasures has remained both secure and obscure in the vaults of the University of Colorado Library's Rare Books Room. Except for the local Slavic scholars and a few specialists in the works of Boris Pasternak, it slumbered quietly, unread and unrecognized. It contains volumes written in most of the Slavic languages, both ancient and modern; in addition, Latin and modern European tongues are represented. Gifts received over a period of several years from Professor Eugene M. Kayden form its nucleus, many coming from his family's home in Russia. Other important additions were made by the late Professor S. Harrison Thomson, medievalist and historian, by Professor Eugene Petriwsky of the Library's faculty, and most recently—through Professor Petriwsky's acumen—the library of Professor Thomas Riha.

Professor Petriwsky and I decided to compile this catalogue some years ago when we discovered a mutual interest—the rare Slavica resting in the locked stacks of Special Collections. Professor Petriwsky's background includes economics degrees from the Universities of Tuebingen and St. Gallen, a master of arts degree from the University of Denver, and a doctor of philosophy degree in Slavic literatures from the Ukrainian Free University, Munich. He is presently assistant director of the University of Colorado Libraries in charge of collection assessment and development. I have been associated with the Special Collections Department of the University of Colorado Libraries for eleven years and served part of that time as acting head. A bachelor of arts in art history, years of omnivorous reading, ballet and modern dancing, and book reviewing have prepared me for life among rare books.

The compilers of this catalogue reach out to you, our readers, with what we hope will be a valuable tool and a source for further Slavic scholarship.

SONIA L. JACOBS

EUGENE MARK KAYDEN
AN APPRECIATION

EUGENE KAYDEN would have been one hundred years old in 1986. He died in his ninety-first year, frail, yet overflowing with plans for unwritten books and unfinished projects. At whatever his age, in whatever his state of health, he radiated a fiery philosophy that will persist as long as caring people of all nations continue to read poetry in the language of its origin or in translation. In a 1974 letter, Kayden expressed his philosophy—

> In the past, religion was the cement creating ethical affirmations and inhibitions; today Art must serve as the link between nations and races. . . . It is my fundamental philosophy that I am a "guest" in this world, to use a line from Akhmatova, that I owe everything to centuries of human civilization and that I must repay that large burden of debt in my own lifetime. . . . I want to give all I have to the cause of the new and the living future. . . .[1]

At the University of Colorado, Eugene Kayden's goal reached fulfillment. He gave monies to set up an endowment fostering literary translations as well as original works; he gave the best of his own, treasured library to the University Libraries, some of which had been gathered by his family in Russia and which dated from the nineteenth century; and most important, he gave of himself, a world-acclaimed translator of Russian literature.

His "lifetime of hard work [required] sacrifice and congeniality."[2] As the translator of Pushkin and other Russian literary luminaries, he "performed a real and splendid service to posterity."[3] "He . . . would . . . rank among the best translators of Russian verse in English [combining] the two qualities most needed in a translator—a perfect command of both languages and definite

Eugene M. Kayden
while "a 'guest' in this
world": (top right)
New York, 1908, five
years after his arrival
in the United States;
(lower left) a middle-
aged professor of eco-
nomics in Sewanee,
Tennessee; (lower
right) contemplating
retirement from the
University of the
South and commence-
ment of a new career.

poetic talent of his own."[4] "It is now his [Boris Pasternak's] good fortune to have found a translator . . . who can handle his 'figurative tendency' in English without doing violence to the poet's own unique view of the world. The reader . . . will get an extraordinarily faithful version of the ideas and feeling of Russia's great modern poet. . . . Many of the shorter poems do not betray their origin in another language."[5] How was this small, intensely serious, quite formal, and sometimes gruff professor and chairman of the Economics Department at the University of the South in Sewanee, Tennessee, able to attain his "aim of building a verbal bridge of understanding between the two cultures"?[6] Why was the University of Colorado held in affectionate esteem?

He was born and educated in Russia. "I had no English when I came to the States in October 1903. I was sixteen then, a teenager who never worked for a living. I had one suitcase containing a pair of pants, two shirts, two suits of underwear, four of my mother's prize face towels, and six books of Russian poetry, the classics in one-volume editions. In the Fall of 1908 I appeared in Boulder with $35.00. I worked my way through college as draftsman . . . as furnace man . . . at anything."[7] Several University of Colorado professors became interested in the immigrant student (an uncommon figure at the then small, unsophisticated state university) and inspired him to start translating Russian poetry. It was a task which would help Kayden in his study of English, and it would be useful in widening the understanding of his peers of a language and culture foreign to the mountain west. In a class on Greek literature in translation, as an exercise in proving certain theories regarding epic poetry composition, Kayden was encouraged to translate into prose his "first love,"[8] Mihkail Lermontov. He chose *The Song of Tsar Ivan the Dreadful and the Merchant Kalashnikov,* succeeding so well that "Dr. Norlin honored me by having me read the poem in his class."[9] *Poet Lore,* a prestigious literary magazine, published the translation in 1913.

Eugene Kayden was a busy student. The 1912 yearbook, *The Coloradoan*, lists "Cap" as an entrant in the Oratorical Prohibition Contest, as a member (and president) of the Social Science Club, as a member of the Historical Club and the Debating Society, and as a reporter on two campus publications. One month after graduating with a bachelor of arts degree in May 1912, Eugene Mark Kayden received certificate No. 38643 as an American citizen. Dean Fleming of the School of Law was his sponsor.

Kayden left Boulder for Cambridge, Massachusetts, with $75 in his pocket and a Harvard Fellowship. He completed his master of arts degree at Harvard in 1913. Further graduate work at Princeton and Columbia Universities, along with instructorships in both economics and English followed. But, in 1917, his graduate work was interrupted when the United States entered into World War I. He became a full-time economist and trade expert, first for the Department of State and later for the Department of Agriculture. By 1923 he was ready to accept an appointment from the University of the South, where he was described as "one of the greatest teachers Sewanee ever had."[10] Kayden's energies focused on economics for thirty-two years before his "retirement" in 1955. He never married. His entire life was devoted to his academic studies, and Russian poetry was something he shared with a few friends in private moments.

His retirement from teaching marked the beginning of an outstanding literary career devoted to the writing and publishing of highly lauded translations of Pushkin, Lermontov, Pasternak, and other Russian writers. Only death ended his enthusiasm for this project of his later years. Kayden's lofty literary standards coupled with his humanitarianism earned him honorary doctorates at the University of the South and at his beloved University of Colorado. His inspired writing paralleled his life-long belief that a nation's soul shone through its literature.

This catalogue, *Rare Books Slavica in the University of Colorado Libraries,* is dedicated to Eugene Mark Kayden, whose gifts have made its publication possible. We hope that it will function as a signpost guiding Earth's "guests" along the route linking nations and races.

[1] Eugene M. Kayden, letter to Ellsworth Mason, July 1, 1974. Special Collections Department, University of Colorado.

[2] Eugene M. Kayden, letter to Dr. J.J. Bennett, Vice Chancellor, University of the South.

[3] Maurice Bowra, letter to E.M. Kayden, June 6, 1963.

[4] Ernest J. Simmons, Columbia University (cited by E.M. Kayden).

[5] Joseph Barnes, editor, Simon & Schuster, *Sewanee Review*, Spring 1960.

[6] *Colorado Quarterly*, Winter 1971, xix, 3, 305–6.

[7] E.M. Kayden, letter to Henry Waltemade, April 9, 1968.

[8] E.M. Kayden, letter to Henry Waltemade, August 13, 1969.

[9] *Ibid.*

[10] Dean Bruton, University of the South, 1969.

RARE BOOKS SLAVICA
IN THE
UNIVERSITY OF COLORADO
LIBRARIES

1. Afanas'ev, Aleksandr N. *Russian Secret Tales.* Bawdy Folktales of Old Russia. Folklore annotations by Giuseppe Pitre. Introduction by G. Legman. Illustrations and decorations by Leon Kotkofsky. New York: Brussel and Brussel, 1966. xix, 306 pp.; illus.

2. Afanas'ev, Nikolai I. *Sovremenniki: al'bom biografii* [Contemporaries: A Collection of Biographies]. S.-Peterburg: Tip. A.S. Suvorina, 19—. illus.
    Library has volume 2 only (1910).

3. Akhmatova, Anna A. *Belaia staia: stikhotvoreniia* [White Flock: Poems]. 2. izd. S.-Peterburg: Izd-vo Prometei N.N. Mikhailova, 1918. 135 pp.

4. Aksakov, Ivan S. *Biografiia Fedora Ivanovicha Tiutcheva* [Fedor Tiutchev, a Biography]. Moskva: Tip. M.G. Volchaninova, 1886. 327 pp.; illus.

5. Aldanov, Mark A. *Iunost' Pavla Stroganova i drugie kharakteristiki* [Pavel Stroganov's Youth and Other Character Sketches]. Belgrade: Izdatel'skaia komissiia, [1935(?)]. 188 pp.

6. Aldanov, Mark A. *Punshevaia vodka i mogila voina* [Vodka Punch and a Warrior's Grave]. Parizh: Dom knigi, 1940. 294 pp.
    Author's autographed presentation copy.

7. Aldanov, Mark A. *Sovremenniki* [Contemporaries]. Berlin: Slovo, 1928. 269 pp.

8. Aldanov, Mark A. *Zagovor* [Conspiracy]. Berlin: Slovo, 1927. 445 pp.

    Author's autographed presentation copy.

9. *Aleksandr I i dvienadtsatyi god* [Alexander I and the Year 1812]. Album. S.-Peterburg?: [19—].

    Ink drawings of the subjects, including Russian military uniforms of the Franco-Russian War.

10. Aleksandrov, A. *Polnyi anglo-russkii slovar'* [Complete English-Russian Dictionary]. Izd. 2. ispr. i dop. S.-Peterburg: Glav. skl. Glavnago Shtaba, 1891. 7, 865, 9, 4 pp.

    In 1974, Eugene Kayden wrote that his brother gave him the dictionary in 1904 to "speed up" his study of English.

11. *Al'manakh sovremennykh russkikh gosudarstvennykh dieiatelei* [Almanac of Contemporary Russian Government Leaders]. Izd. Germana A. Goldberga. S.-Peterburg: Tip. Isidora Goldberga, 1897. xxxix, 1,250 pp.

12. Andersen, Hans Christian. *Mat': skazka Gansa Khristiana Andersena na dvadtsati dvukh iazykakh* [Mother: a Tale in Twenty-Two Languages]. S portretom avtora, gravirovannym po derevie V. Mate. Risunok oblozhki M. Dal'kevicha. Izdal P. Ganzen. S.-Peterburg: Tip. S.M. Nikolaeva, 1894. vii, 144 pp.

    Added to title page: *Une mère.*

13. Andreev, Leonid N. *P'esy* [Plays]. Vstup. stat'ia i obshchaia red. A. Dimshitsa. Sostavlenie, podgotovka tekstov i primechaniia V. Chubakova. Moskva: Iskusstvo, 1959. 589 pp.; illus.

14. Andreev, Leonid N. *Tsar' Golod. Predstavlenie v piati kartinakh s prologom* [King Hunger]. Berlin: Bühnen-und Buchverlag russischer Autoren. T. Ladyschnikow, 1908. 95 pp.

15a. Andreev, Leonid N. *King Hunger.* Translated by Eugene M. Kayden. Boston: Poet Lore, 1911. In *Poet Lore*, v. 22, no. 6, winter 1911. pp. 401–459.

> A bound copy of the magazine, published by Richard G. Gadger, Boston, in a series entitled *Poet Lore Plays.* Inscribed as follows:
> "Greetings! To the Library of the University of Colorado to its special collection of poor but rare translations, with my compliments! I translated *King Hunger* in 1908 and had it published in 1911. It bears all the earmarks of my immaturity in the use of English. I hope to publish a new revision edition.
>
> Eugene M. Kayden
28 April 1967"

15b. Andreev, Leonid N. *King Hunger.* Translated by Eugene M. Kayden. Second American revision. Sewanee, Tenn.: University Press, University of the South, 1973. xii, 110 pp.

> Eugene Kayden inscribed this book to Norlin Library. H.H. Arnold of the University of Colorado Foundation wrote the following to Dr. Ellsworth Mason, Director of the Libraries, on June 29, 1973: "For your information, Professor Kayden first translated *King Hunger* while attending the University of Colorado between 1908 and 1912 as a means of practicing his English. His translation was so well done that it was published in the quarterly *Poet Lore* in 1911. President Norlin, among others, encouraged Professor Kayden to continue to translate the works of Russian poets because of his obvious talents."
>
> Eugene Kayden gave the University of Colorado the original one-page typed letter and envelope which confirmed his debut in an American periodical as a translator. It was dated 1 February, 1912. *Poet Lore* published the play in its winter edition of 1911. The letter tells the young undergraduate that all rights of production of the play belong to him.

16. Antokol'skii, Pavel G. *O Pushkine* [On Pushkin]. Moscow: Sov. pisatel', 1960. 136 pp.

17. *Apollon.* okt. 1909 -okt./dek. 1917. Petrograd, S.-Peterburg. Illus. Library holdings incomplete.

   The leading literary and art magazine for the cultured reader in S.-Peterburg.

18. *Artisty Moskovskago khudozhestvennago teatra za rubezhom* [Actors of the Moscow Arts Theater Abroad]. Praga: Nasha riech, 1922. 62 pp.; illus.

19. Artzybasheff, Boris M. *Seven Simeons.* A Russian tale retold and illustrated by Boris Artzybasheff. New York: Viking Press, 1937. 31 pp.; col. illus.

20. Atkinson, Thomas W. *Oriental and Western Siberia, a Narrative of Seven Years Explorations and Adventures in Siberia, Mongolia, The Kirghis Steppes, Chinese Tartary, and Part of Central Asia.* London: Hurst and Blackett, successors to Henry Cobburn, 1858. 611, 23 pp.; illus. (some col.).

21. Atkinson, Thomas W. *Travels in the Regions of the Upper and Lower Amoor and the Russian Acquisitions on the Confines of India and China.* With Adventures Among the Mountain Kirghis; and the Manjours, Manyargs, Toungous, Touzemts, Goldi and Gelyaks; the Hunting and Pastoral Tribes. New York: Harper, 1860. xii, 448, 4 pp.; illus., map.

22. *Aucassin et Nicolette.* Aucassin and Nicolete in English, by Andrew Lang. Praha: Státní tiskárna, 1931. 77 pp.; col. illus.
   Printed for the Limited Editions Club. No. 1,250/1,500. Signed by Vojtech Preissig, the designer and illustrator.

23. Bain, Robert N. *Cossack Fairy Tales and Folk-Tales.* With illustrations by E.W. Mitchell. New York: A.L. Burt, 1894. viii (i.e. x), 356 pp.; illus.

В. А. Сѣровъ. Портретъ Шаляпина (рисунокъ углемъ и мѣломъ, 1896—1897). (Собств. Ѳ. И. Шаляпина).

V. Séroff. Portrait de Chaliapine (charbon et craie). (App. à M. Th. Chaliapine).

Portrait of F. Chaliapin by V. Seroff, in charcoal
and crayon, from *Apollon*, September 1914. (No. 17)

24. Bainbridge, Henry C. *Peter Carl Fabergé, Goldsmith and Jeweller to the Russian Imperial Court and the Principal Crowned Heads of Europe*. An Illustrated Record and Review of His Life and Work, A.D. 1846–1920. Foreword by Sacheverell Sitwell. London: B.T. Batsford, 1949. 169 pp.; illus.

25. Bakst, Léon. *The Designs of Léon Bakst for "The Sleeping Princess."* A Ballet in Five Acts after Perrault, Music by Tchaikovsky. Preface by André Levinson. London: Benn Bros., 1923. 18 pp.; illus.
    No. 141/1000. *See also* Levinson, A.I., No. 217.

26. Bal'mont, Konstantin D. *Golubaia Podkova: stikhi o Sibiri* [A Blue Horseshoe: Poems about Siberia]. Southbury, Conn.: Atlas, [n.d.] 44 pp.; illus.
    Signed, holograph verse by author on title page.

27. Bal'mont, Konstantin D. *Iz mirovoi poezii* [From World Poetry]. Berlin: Slovo, 1921. 200 pp.

28. Barto, Agnia L. *Toy-Time*. Translated by Herbert Marshall. Drawings by K. Kouznetsov. Moscow: Mejdunarodnaya Kniga, [194–?]. 12 pp.; illus. (some col.).

29. Basina, Marianna I. *Tam, gde shumiat mikhailovskie roshchi* [Where the Murmur of the Mikhailovsky Groves Is Heard]. Leningrad: Gos. Izd-vo detskoi lit-ry, 1962. 286 pp.; illus.

30. Belinskii, Vissarion G. *Izbrannyia sochineniia* [Selected Works]. 2. izd. S.-Peterburg: Izd. Akts. obshch. tip. Diela, 1911- v.-. Illus.
    Library has volume 1.

31. Ben-Iakov, Bronila. *Slovar' Argo GULaga* [Dictionary of Gulag Lingo]. Frankfurt/Main: Posev, 1982. 149 pp.

К. Д. БАЛЬМОНТЪ.

Какъ Вы, люблю я орхидею,
Какъ Вы, люблю, любя любить.
Но вдругъ запутался я въ ней,
Ее распутать — не умѣю.

ГОЛУБАЯ ПОДКОВА

Вотъ — орхидея предо мной,
Но какъ къ ней подойти, не знаю,
И вовсе близокъ сердцемъ къ Раю,

СТИХИ О СИБИРИ.

Но въ сердцѣ — только адскій зной...
Прильнуть бы къ влагѣ неземной!

К. Бальмонтъ.

1935. 25 апрѣля.
Парижъ.

ALATAS
SOUTHBURY, CONN.
U. S. A.

Holograph verse, signed by the author on title
page of K.D. Balmont's *Golubaia podkova.* (No. 26)

32. Beneš, Eduard. *The Moral Crisis in Europe*. 18 pp. typescript, signed and inscribed to the University of Colorado. This commencement address was delivered in Boulder, June 1939.

> One page letter, typed, laid in and signed by E.B. Hitchcock, Dr. Beneš's personal aide. Addressed to President George Norlin of the University of Colorado and dated July 11, 1939, letter conveys manuscript of Beneš's address to the university archives.
> *See also*: Masaryk, Tomaš G., No. 241.

33. Bible (Russian). *Bibliia ili kniga sveshchennago pisaniia Vetkhago i Novago Zavieta*. Izd. 2. Sanktpeterburg: V Sinodal'noi tip., 1878. 1600, 392 pp.

34. Bible. O.T. (Church Slavic). *Kievskaia Psaltir' 1397 goda* [Kievan Psalter]. Moskva: Iskusstvo, 1978. 229 leaves; col. illus. facsimile edition.

> *See also* Vzdornov, G.I., No. 446.

35. Bible. O.T. (Hebrew). *Torah*. Warschau: M. Scholtz, [18—?] 605 pp.

> A miniature Old Testament, 1 3/16 x 13/16 x 9/32 inches. In a silver case with a magnifying glass inset, this Bible belonged to Eugene Kayden's father.

36. Bible. N.T. (Church Slavic). *Assemanov ili Vatikanski evangelistar*. Iznesé ga na svjetlo Franjo Rački. U Zagrebu: Sloví A. Jakiča, 1865. cxix, 216 pp.; illus.

37. Bible. N.T. (Church Slavic). *Codex Assemanus*. Evangeliarium Assemani, Codex Vaticanus 3. Slavicus Glag. Editio phototypica cum prolegomenis, textu litteris Cyrillicis transcripto, analysi, annotationibus palaeographicis, variis lectionibus, glossario. Ediderunt Jos. Vajs, Jos. Kurz. Pragae: Sumptibus Academiae Scientiarium et Artium Bohemicae, 1929–55. 2 v.; illus.

38. Bible. N.T. (Czech). *Nový Zákon z roku 1475.* V. Praze: 1930. Fascimile edition. 418 pp.

39. Bible. N.T. (Polish). *Pismo Święte Nowego Testamentu.* Nowy przekład z Wulgaty. Komentarz przez Eugeniusza Dąbrowskiego. Warszawa: Pax, 1953. 876 pp.; maps.

40. Bible. N.T. (Ukrainian). *Chytannia apostol's'ki na nedili, praznyky i rizni potreby.* Peredslovo Verkhovnoho arkhyiepyskopa i kardynala Iosyfa. Rome: 1969. 424 pp.; illus.

41. Bible. N.T. (Ukrainian). *Ievanheliia na nedili, praznyky i rizni potreby.* Peredslovo Verkhovnoho arkhyiepyskopa i kardynala Iosyfa. Rome: 1967. 345 pp.; illus.

42. Bible. N.T. (Ukrainian). *Sviate Ievanheliie.* Visbaden: 1946. 224 (i.e. 449) pp.; illus.
    Reprint of 1938 Warsaw edition.

43. Blagoi, Dmitrii D. *Masterstvo Pushkina* [Pushkin's Literary Genius]. Moskva: Sov. pisatel', 1955. 265 pp.

44. Bloch, Marie H. *Ivanko and the Dragon.* An Old Ukrainian Folk Tale. From the Original Collection of Ivan Rudchenko. Illustrations by Yaroslava. New York: Atheneum, 1969. Unpaginated; col. illus.

45. Bloch, Marie H. *Ukrainian Folk Tales.* From the Original Collections of Ivan Rudchenko and Maria Lukiyanenko. Illustrated by J. Hnizdovsky. New York: Coward-McCann, 1964. 77 pp.; illus.

46. Blok, Aleksandr A. *Dvienadtsat'* [The Twelve]. Risunki Iu. Annenkova. Peterburg: Alkonost, 1918. 62 pp.; illus.

Title page illustration by I. Annenkov
from A.A. Blok's *Dvienadtsat'*. (No. 46)

47. Blumenthal, Verra X. *Folk Tales from the Russian*. Chicago: Rand, McNally, 1903. 153 pp.; illus.

48. Boccaccio, Giovanni. *Welmi piekna nowa kronika / a neb historia / wo welike milosti / kniežete a kraale Floria z Hispanij / a geho milee pānie Baintzeforze* [Tales]. Wam znij welike potiessenie przigde yakž srozumiete kterak welike zalijbenij milost maa / S vtiessenymi ffigurami. W. Praze: Tisstiena skrze Jana Ssmerhovskeho, 1519. cxiiii pp.; illus.
　　Facsimile edition. V Praze: Tiskem Čsl. kompasu, 1928.

49. Botlin, Ivan N. *Primechaniia na Istoriiu drevniia i nynieshniia Rossii g. Leklerka* [Notes on the History of Ancient and Modern Russia by Monsieur Leclerc]. S.-Peterburg: Tip. Gornago Uchilishcha, 1788. 2 v.

50. Bourke-White, Margaret. *Shooting the Russian War*. Written and photographed by Margaret Bourke-White. New York: Simon and Schuster, 1942. xiv, 208 pp.; illus.
　　See also: Caldwell, Erskine; Fischer, Louis.

51. Bowring, John. *Specimens of the Polish Poets*. With notes and observations on the literature of Poland. London: Printed by the author, sold by Baldwin, Cradock, and Joy, 1827. 227 pp.; folded sheet (music).

52. Bowring, John. *Specimens of the Russian Poets*. With preliminary remarks and biographical notices. Second edition with additions. London: 1821–23. 2 v.

53. Brand, Adam. *À Journal of the Embassy From . . . John and Peter Alexievitz, Emperors of Muscovy, &c. Over Land into China . . . to Peking . . . By Everard Isbrand, Their Ambassador in the Years 1693, 1694, and 1695*. Translated from the Original in High-

Dutch. To which is added Curious Observations concerning the Products of Russia by H. W. Ludolf. London: D. Brown, 1698. 134 pp.; illus.

54. Brodskii, Nikolai L. *Literaturnye salony i kruzhki: pervaia polovina XIX veka* [Literary Salons and Circles; First Half of the Nineteenth Century]. Moskva: Academia, 1930. xxi, 592 pp.; illus.

55. Brown[e], Edward. *A Brief Account Of Some Travels In divers Parts of Europe, Viz. Hungaria, Servia, Bulgaria, Macedonia, Thessaly, Austria, Styria, Carinthia, Carniola, and Friuli.* Through a great part of Germany, And The Low Countries. Through Marca Trevisana, and Lombardy on both sides the Po. With some Observations on the Gold, Silver, Copper, Quick-silver Mines, and the Baths and Mineral Waters in those Parts. As Also, The Description of many Antiquities, Habits, Fortifications and Remarkable Places. The Second Edition with many Additions. London: Printed for Benj. Tooke, at the Sign of the Ship in St. Paul's Church-yard, 1685. 222, 4 pp.; illus.

56. Brückner, Alexander. *Illiustrirovannaia istoriia Petra Velikago* [Illustrated History of Peter the Great]. S.-Peterburg: Izd. P.P. Soikina, 1902. 2 v. in 1; illus.

57. Bunin, Ivan A. *The Gentleman from San Francisco, and Other Stories.* Translated from the Russian by S.S. Koteliansky and Leonard Woolf. Richmond, England: Published by Leonard and Virginia Woolf at the Hogarth Press, 1922. v, 86 pp.

58. Bunin, Ivan A. *The Gentleman from San Francisco, and Other Stories.* Translated from the Russian by D.H. Lawrence, S.S. Koteliansky, and Leonard Woolf. Second edition. London: Published by Leonard and Virginia Woolf at the Hogarth Press, 1934. v, 86 pp.

59. Burliuk, David D. *Entelekhizm: teoriia, kritika, stikhi, kartiny, 1907–1930;* K 20ti-letiiu futurisma [Entelechy: Theory, Criticism, Poems, Canvases, 1907–1930]. New York: M.N. Burliuk, 1930. 24 pp.

> An inscription in *Entelekhi* reads: "Dorogomu i glubokochtimomu velikomu drugu i khudozhniku S. Iu. Sudeikinu. David Burliuk. [To dear and deeply respected great friend and artist S. Iu. Sudeikin. David Burliuk.] The title page has the inscription: "Father of Russian Proletarian Futurism David Burliuk."

60. Byval'kevich, M.G. *Verki; istoricheskii etiud* [Verki; An Historic Study]. Ottisk iz "Vilenskago viestnika". Vil'na: Tip. A.G. Sirkina, 1895. 12 pp.

61. Caldwell, Erskine. *North of the Danube.* Photographs by Margaret Bourke-White. New York: Viking Press, [1939]. 128, 8 pp.

62. Carroll, Lewis. *Alice in Wonderland.* Translated by V. Sirin [Vladimir Nabokov] with drawings by S. Zalshupin. New York: Dover, 1976. 114, 7 pp.

63. Carroll, Lewis. *The Russian Journal and Other Selections from the Works of Lewis Carroll.* Edited with an introduction by John Francis McDermott. New York: E.P. Dutton, 1935. 252 pp.

64. Castera, Jean H. *Vie de Catherine II, Impératrice de Russie.* Avec six Portraits gravés en taille-douce. Paris: Chez F. Buisson, 1797. 2 v.; illus.

65. Čelakovsky, František L. *Wothłós pěsni russkich* [Echoes from Russian Songs]. Do łužisko-serbskje rečje přełožištaj J.E. Smoler a J.A. Wařko. Prazy: n.p., 1846. 70 pp.

66. Celli, Rose. *Baba Yaga, a Popular Russian Tale.* Translated by Katharine Hawley. Illustrated by Nathalie Parain. Planned by Père Castor. Poughkeepsie: Artists' and Writers' Guild, 1935. 16 pp.; col. illus.

67. Chaplina, Vera. *Zoo Babies.* Translated from the Russian by Ivy Litvinov. Illustrated by D. Gorlov. Moscow: Foreign Languages Publishing House, [1950?]. 207 pp.; illus.

68. Chaplina, Vera. *Scamp and Crybaby.* Translated by Ivy Litvinov. Photographs by A. Anzhanov. Moscow: Foreign Languages Publishing House, 1961. 22, 2 pp.

69. Chekhov, Anton P. *Two Plays: The Cherry Orchard and Three Sisters.* With an introduction by John Gielgud and illustrations by Lajos Szalay. Translated by Constance Garnett. New York: Thistle Press, 1966. xvi, 152 pp.; illus. (some col.).
> Published for the Limited Editions Club. No. 12/1500. Signed by Lajos Szalay.

70. Chelčický, Petr. *Siet wiery* [System of Faith]. Na Klassterze Wylemowskem. Praha: Tisk. Neuber, Pour, 1926. ccxxxvi pp.; illus.
> Facsimile edition of 1521 title.

71. Cherepov, Ivan A. *Alpinisme soviètique.* Traduit du russe par Paul Sulfourt. Paris: Amiot-Dumont, 1957. 201 pp.; illus.

72. *Children's Drawings and Poems, Terezin, 1942–1944.* Edited by Hana Volavkova. Translated into English by Jeanne Nemcova. First edition. Praha: 1959. 80 pp.; illlus., (some col.).
> Drawings from the State Jewish Museum in Prague.

73. Chinnov, Igor. *Kompozitsiia* [Composition]. Piataia kniga stikhov. Parizh: Rifma, 1972. 116 pp.

An edition of 300. Russian inscription to Professor E.M. Kayden by the author.

74. Chinnov, Igor. *Linii* [Lines]. Vtoraia kniga stikhov. Parizh: Rifma, 1960. 58 pp.

An edition of 350.

75. Chinnov, Igor. *Metafory* [Metaphors]. N'iu-Iork: Izd-vo Novogo zhurnala, 1968. 51 pp.

An edition of 600.

76. Chinnov, Igor. *Partitura*. N'iu-Iork: Novyi zhurnal, 1970. 50 pp.

An edition of 500. Inscribed in English: "To Professor Eugene M. Kayden, Lover and Translator of Russian Poetry, from Igor Chinnov." In a letter dated July 5, 1974, Kayden wrote, "Igor Chinnov [is] one of the best known Russian emigré poets, who will be studied and translated before long."

77. Chodźko, Aleksander. *Fairy Tales of the Slav Peasants and Herdsmen*. Translated from the French and illustrated by Emily J. Harding. London: George Allen, 1896. 327 pp.

78. Chodźko, Aleksander. *Slav Fairy Tales of the Slav Peasants and Herdsmen*. Translated from the French and profusely illustrated by Emily J. Harding. New York: A.L. Burt, [1899?]. 327 pp.; illus.

79. Chukovskii, Kornei I. *Wash'em Clean*. Drawings by Kanevsky. Moscow: Foreign Languages Publishing House, [n.d.]. 24 pp.

80. Chukovskii, Kornei I. *Skazki* [Fairy Tales]. Risunki Vl. Konashevicha. Moskva: Academia, 1935. 158, 6 pp.

81. Chukovskii, Kornei I. *Sovremenniki; portrety i etiudy* [Contemporaries; Portraits and Studies]. Izd. 4. ispr. i dop. Moskva: Molodaia gvardiia, 1967. 588 pp.; illus.

> In a letter dated May 1, 1968, Eugene Kayden wrote to the University of Colorado Librarian: "Chukovsky is prominent as a critic and poet. This copy bears the following presentation: To Professor E. Kayden heartfelt greetings from Kornei Chukovsky 7/X/67 Peredelkino. Chukovsky was a neighbor of Pasternak at Peredelkino, a suburb of Moscow."

82. *Constitution (Fundamental Law) of the Union of the Soviet Socialist Republics.* New York: The National Council of American-Soviet Friendship, 1941. 39, 1 pp.; double map.

> An English-language text of Stalin's constitution, adopted in 1937.

83. Conquest, Robert. *The Harvest of Sorrow: Soviet Collectivization and the Terror Famine.* New York: Oxford University Press, 1986. 412 pp.; illus.

> Author's autographed presentation copy.

84. Čop, Jaka. *Svet med vrhovi; Julijske Alpe. The World Among the Summits; The Julian Alps.* Ljubljana: Državna založba Slovenije, 1962. 244 pp.; illus.

85. Cosmas, of Prague. *Chronicae Bohemorum libri III, in quibus gentis origo et prisciduces usque ad Wratislaum primum regem creatum sub Henrico III,* imp. & annum Christi MCXXVII. Nunc primum integre in lucem edit. Item S. Adalberti episcop Pragenis vita et martyrivm ab eodene Cosma decano descripta. Praefixa ducum regumque Bohemia elogia versibus decantata a Martino Cutheno et Caspare Cropacio, Poetis Bohemis. Hanoviae: Claudius Marnius et Io. Aubrii, 1607. 12, 84 pp.; 2 v. in 1.

COSMÆ
PRAGENSIS
ECCLESIÆ DECANI
CHRONICÆ BOHEMORVM
Libri III,

Jn quibus gentis origo, & prisci Duces, vsque ad Wratislaum
primum Regem creatum sub HENRICO III. Imp.
& annum Christi MCXXVI.

Nunc primum integrè in lucem editi.

Item

S. ADALBERTI EPISCOPI
PRAGENSIS VITA ET MARTYRIVM
ab eodem COSMA DECANO descripta.

PRAEFIXA DVCVM REGVMQ. BOHEMIAE ELOGIA
versibus decantata à MARTINO CVTHENO & CASPARE
CROPACIO, *Poetis Bohemis.*

HANOVIÆ,
Typis Wechelianis, apud Claudium Marnium
& heredes Ioannis Aubrii.

Title page, *Chronicae Bohemorum libri
III.* by Cosmas of Prague. (No. 85)

17

86. *Costume of the Russian Empire*. Illustrated by Upwards of Seventy Richly Coloured Engravings. London: Printed by T. Bensley for J. Stockdale, 1811. 154 pp.; 72 col. illus.

87. Cottin, Marie (Risteau) called Sophie. *Elizabeth or, the Exiles of Siberia*. A tale founded upon facts. New York: Kiggins & Kellogg, [18—]. vi, 128 pp.; illus.

88. Cottin, Marie (Risteau) called Sophie. *Elizabeth; or, The Exiles of Siberia*. A tale founded upon facts. From the French of Madame Cottin. Philadelphia: Printed by Jane Aitkin for Mathew Carey, 1814. iv, 166 pp.; illus.

89. Coxe, William. *Account of the Russian Discoveries Between Asia and America*. To Which are Added, the Conquest of Siberia, and The History of the Transactions and Commerce between Russia and China. Revised and corrected third edition. London: Printed by J. Nichols for T. Cadell in the Strand, 1787. xxviii, 454 pp.; folded maps.

90. Ćurčija-Prodanović, Nada. *Yugoslav Folk Tales*. Illustrated by Joan Kiddell-Monroe. London: Oxford University Press, 1957. 210 pp.; illus.

91. Dal', Vladimir I. *Tolkovyi slovar' zhivago velikorusskago iazyka* [Defining Dictionary of the Great Russian Language]. 2.izd., ispr. i znachitel'no umnozhennoe po rukopisi avtora. S.-Peterburg: Izdanie knigoprodavtsa - tipografa N.D. Vol'fa, 1880–1882. 4 v.
The most important dictionary used by Russian language specialists.

92. Darskii, Dmitrii S. *"Chudesnye vymysly." O kosmicheskom soznanii v lirike Tiutcheva* [Miraculous Inventions. On the Cosmic Consciousness in Tiutchev's Lyric Poetry]. Moskva: T-vo skoropechatni A.A. Levensona, 1913, cover 1914. x, 136 pp.

93. Darskii, Dmitrii S. *Radost' zemli: issledovanie liriki Feta* [Earthly Happiness: an Investigation of Fet's Lyric Poetry]. Moskva: Izd-vo K. F. Nekrasova, 1916. 207 pp.

94. D'iachenko, Grigorii M. *Polnyi tserkovno-slavianskii slovar'* [Complete Church-Slavonic Dictionary]. So vneseniem v nego vazhnieishikh drevne-russkikh slov i vyrazhenii. Vsiekh slov ob'iasneno okolo 30,000. Moskva: Tip. Vil'de, 1899. xxxviii, 1,120 pp.

95. Dirr, Adolf. *Caucasian Folk-Tales.* Translated into English by Lucy Menzies. New York: E.P. Dutton, 1929. xiii, 306 pp.

96. Dobson, George. *Russia Painted by F. de Haenen.* Text by G. Dobson, H. M. Grove, and H. Stewart. London: A. and C. Black, 1913. x, 479 pp.; illus. (some col.), map.

97. Dostoevskii, Fedor M. *The Brothers Karamazov.* A novel in four parts and epilogue. Translated by Constance Garnett; revised with an introduction by Avrahm Yarmolinsky. Eighteen portraits by Alexander King. Boston: Limited Editions Club, 1933. 3 v.; illus.
   No. 1250/1500. Signed by Alexander King.

98. Dostoevskii, Fedor M. *The Brothers Karamazov.* A novel in four parts and epilog. Translated by Constance Garnett; revised with an introduction by Avrahm Yarmolinsky. Illustrated with lithographs by Fritz Eichenberg. New York: Limited Editions Club, 1949. 2 v.; illlus.
   No. 713/1500. Signed by Fritz Eichenberg.

99. Dostoevskii, Fedor M. *Crime & châtiment; drame en sept tableaux.* Représenté pour la première fois à Paris, sur le Théâtre

National de l'Odéon, le samedi 15 septembre 1888. Paris: 1888.
88 pp.

100. Dostoevskii, Fedor M. *Crime and Punishment.* Translated by
Constance Garnett with an introduction by Laurence Irving and
illustrated with wood-engravings by Fritz Eichenberg. New York:
Limited Editions Club, 1948. 2 v.; illus.
> No. 434/1500. Signed by Fritz Eichenberg.

101. Dostoevskii, Fedor M. *The Gambler, and Notes from Under-
ground.* Translated by Constance Garnett, introduction by George
Steiner, illustrated by Alexandre Alexeieff. Bloomfield, Connect-
icut: Sign of the Stone Book, 1967. xv, 352, 5 pp.; illus.
> Printed for the Limited Editions Club. No. 12/1500. Signed by A.
> Alexeieff.

102. Dostoevskii, Fedor M. *The Idiot.* A novel in four parts.
Translated by Constance Garnett with an introduction by Avrahm
Yarmolinsky and illustrated with wood-engravings by Fritz Eichen-
berg. New York: Limited Editions Club, 1956. xvi, 560 pp.; illus.
> No. 434/1500. Signed by Fritz Eichenberg.

103. Dostoevskii, Fedor M. *The Possessed.* Translated by Constance
Garnett with an introduction by Marc Slonim. Including the
suppressed chapter, "Stavrogin's Confession." Translated by Avrahm
Yarmolinsky and illustrated by Fritz Eichenberg. Hartford, Con-
necticut: Case, Lockwood and Brainard, 1959. 2 v.; illus.
> Printed for the Limited Editions Club. No. 1,149/1,500. Signed by
> Fritz Eichenberg.

104. Downing, Charles. *Russian Tales and Legends.* Illustrated by
Joan Kiddell-Monroe. London: Oxford University Press, 1957. 231
pp.; illus.

105. Dreiser, Theodore. *Dreiser Looks at Russia*. New York: H. Liveright, 1928. 264 pp.; illus.

106. *Drevnerusskaia zhivopis' v sobranii Gosudarstvennoi Tretiakovskoi Galerei* [Ancient Russian Paintings in the Collection of the State Tretiakov Gallery]. Text by Aleksei N. Svirin. Moskva: Gos. izd-vo izobrazitel'nogo iskusstva, 1958. Unpaginated; illus.

107. *Drevnosti Ukrainy* [Ukrainian Antiquities]. Izd. Imp. Moskovskago arkheologicheskago obshchestva. Kiev: Tip. S.V. Kul'zhenko, 1905–. v.-. Illus.
    Library has volume 1.

108. Drummond, David A. *Dictionary of Russian Obscenities*. Second revised edition. Berkeley, Calif.: Berkeley Slavic Specialties, 1980. 79 pp.

109. Duncan, David D. *The Kremlin*. Greenwich, Conn.: New York Graphic Society [1960]. 170 pp.; mounted col. illus.

110. Dunsheath, Joyce. *Guest of the Soviets. Moscow and the Caucasus 1957*. London: Constable, 1959. viii, 183 pp.; illus., map.

111. *26 [Dwadzieścia sześć] współczesnych opowiadań Amerykańskich* [26 Contemporary American Stories]. Wybrał Maxim Lieber. Wyd. 2. Warszawa: Iskry, 1966. 566, 4 pp.

112. *Dziennik Ustaw Rzeczypospolitej Polskiej* [Polish Constitution]. Library has no. 1, 1944; no. 2-58, including index, 1945; no. 1-28, 1946.

113. Efros, Nikolai E. *Moskovskii Khudozhestvennyi teatr, 1898–1923* [Moscow Arts Theater]. Edited by Aleksandr Brodskii. Moskva-Peterburg: Gos. izd-vo, 1924. 148 pp.; illlus., (some col.).

114. Egger, Carl. *Im Kaukasus, Bergbesteigungen und Reiseerlebnisse im Sommer 1914.* Mit 78 Bildern nach Aufnahmen des Verfassers, Kartenskizze und Panorama. Basel: Frobenius, 1915. 144 pp.; illus., maps.

115. Ermilov, Vladimir V. *Fyodor Dostoyevsky, 1821–1881.* Translated from Russian by J. Katzer. Moscow: Foreign Languages Publishing House, [1957?]. 293 pp.; illus.

116. Eschenloer, Peter. *Historia Wratislaviensis et que post mortem regis Ladislai sub electo Georgio de Podiebrat Bohemorum rege illi acciderant prospera et adversa.* Breslau: Joseph Max, 1872.

117. Esipov, Grigorii V. *Raskol'nich'i diela XVIII stolietiia* [Old Believer Affairs of the Eighteenth Century]. Izvlechennyia iz diel Preobrazhenskago prikaza i tainoi rozysknykh diel kantseliarii G. Esipovym. Izd. D. E. Kozhanchikova. Sanktpeterburg: Tip. T-va. "Obshchestvennaia Pol'za," 1861. 654 pp.

118. Evarnyts'kyi, Dmytro I. *Iz ukrainskoi stariny* [From Ukrainian Antiquity]. Risunki S.I. Vasil'kovskago i N.S. Samokisha. Poiasnitel'nyi tekst D.I. Evarnitskago. S. Peterburg: Izd. A.F. Marksa, [1900?]. Varying pagination; col. illus.

119. Evtushenko, Evgenii A. *Invisible Threads.* New York: Macmillan, 1981. 157 pp.; illus. (some col.)
    Author's autographed presentation copy.

120. Evtushenko, Evgenii A. *Selected Poems.* Translated and introduction by Robin Milner-Gulland and Peter Levi. Baltimore: Penguin Books, 1963. 92 pp.

Portrait of H. Skovoroda by S.I. Vasil'kovskii from
D.I. Evarnyts'kyi's *Iz ukrainskoi stariny.* (No. 118)

121. Evtushenko, Evgenii A. *Sobranie sochinenii* [Works]. Moskva: Khudozh. lit-ra, 1983–84. 3 v.
   Author's autographed presentation copy.

122. Fanti, Garaldo. *Dizionario Italiano-Russo*. Bologna: Editrice, Capitol, 1961. 1,015 pp.

123. Favorskii, Vladimir A. *Illustratsii k "Slovu o polku Igoreve"* [Illustrations for the Igor Tale]. Moskva: Izd-vo Akademii khudozhestv SSSR, 1961. 35 pp.; col. illus.

124. Favorskii, Vladimir A. *Slovo o polku Igoreve; graviury.* [The Igor Tale: engravings]. Moskva: Kombinat graficheskogo iskusstva, 1962. Unpaginated; illus.

Fet, Afanasii A. *See* Shenshin, Afanasii A.

125. Fischer, Louis. *Machines and Men in Russia.* Photographs by Margaret Bourke-White. New York: H. Smith, 1932. xv, 283 pp.

126. Filippov, Boris A. *Za tridtsat' let; stikhi, izbrannoe 1941–1971* [Over Thirty Years: Poems 1941–1971]. Washington: 1971. 33 pp.
   Inscribed by the author to Eugene M. Kayden, December 1971.

127. Fillmore, Parker H. *The Shoemaker's Apron; a Second Book of Czechoslovak Fairy Tales and Folk Tales.* Illustrations and decorations by Jan Matulka. New York: Harcourt, Brace, 1920. xiii, 280 pp.; illus. (some col.).

128. Firsoff, Valdemar A. *The Tatra Mountains.* With 65 photographs. London: Lindsay Drummond, 1942. 128 pp.

Illustration for *The Igor Tale*
by V.A. Favorskii. (No. 123)

129. Flegon, Alec. *Vokrug Solzhenitsyna* [Around Solzhenitsyn]. London: Flegon Press, 1981. 2 v.; illus.

130. Flegon, Alec. *Za predelami russkikh slovarei*: dopolnitel'nie slova i znacheniia s tsitatami Lenina, Khrushcheva, Stalina, Barkova, Pushkina, Lermontova, Esenina, Maiakovskogo, Solzhenitsyna, Voznesenskogo. . . . [Beyond the Boundaries of the Russian Dictionaries]. London: Flegon Press, 1973. 413 pp.; illus.
> This work reflects crudity, information, and humor.

131. Fletcher, Giles. *O gosudarstvie russkom ili obraz pravleniia russkago tsaria, obyknovenno nazyvaemago tsarem moskovskim. S opisaniem nravov i obychaev zhitelei etoi strany* [Russia Under the Tsars]. S.-Peterburg: Tipo-litografiia B.M. Vol'fa, 1906. 160 pp.
> Reprint of "V Londonie, pechatano T. D-M dlia Tomasa Charda, 1591 g."
> In a letter dated July 24, 1969, E.M. Kayden notes that this is the first report about Russia by an English traveller. He writes that the book "came from my home library."

132. Ford, Charles H. *The Garden of Disorder and Other Poems.* Introduction by William Carlos Williams with a frontispiece by Pavel Tchelitchew. First edition. London: Europa Press, 1938. 78 pp.; illus.

133. Fortunatov, Filipp F. *Lektsii po fonetikie staroslovianskago (tserkovnoslavianskago) iazyka* [Lectures on the Phonetics of the Old Slavonic (Church Slavonic) Language]. Posmertnoe izd. Petrograd: Izd. Otdieleniia russkago iazyka i slovesnosti Rossiiskoi akademii nauk, 1919. ii, 294 pp.

134. Frank, Semen L. *Etiudy o Pushkine* [Essays on Pushkin]. Munkhen: 1957. 126 pp.

135. Franko, Ivan. *Akordy; antolohiia ukrains'koi liryky vid smerty Shevchenka* [Chords: Anthology of Ukrainian Lyrics After the Death of Shevchenko]. Ilius. Iuliiana Pan'kevycha. U L'vovi: Nakladom Ukrains'ko-rus'koi vyd. s-ky, 1903. 316 pp.; illus.

> Franko, a Ukrainian poet of elegant taste, includes the work of 88 authors in this anthology of Ukrainian lyrical poetry.

136. Freher, Marquard. *Rerum Bohemicarum antiqui scriptores aliquot insignes, partim hactenus incogniti* . . . Accedunt seorsim Ioh. Dubravii . . . Historiae Bohemicae commentarii, longe empendatiores & auctiores. . . . Hanoviae: Typis Wechelianis apud Claudium Marnium, & Heredes Ioannis Aubrii, 1602. 2 v. in 1.

137. Freshfield, Douglas W. *The Exploration of the Caucasus.* With illustrations by Vittorio Sella. London, New York: E. Arnold, 1896. 2 v.; illus., maps.

138. Freshfield, Douglas W. *Travels in the Central Caucasus and Bashan: Including Visits to Ararat and Tabreez and Ascents of Kazbek and Elbruz.* London: Longmans, Green, 1869. Varying pagination; maps.

139. *Glagolita Glozianus; id est Codicis Glagolitici inter suos facile antiquissimi* . . . Dedicavit Bartholomaeus Kopitar. Vindobonae: Prostat apud Carolum Gerold Bibiopolam, 1836. lxxix, 86 pp.

> Printed in the Glagolitic alphabet.

140. Gmelin, Samuel G. *Reise durch Russland zur Untersuchung der drey Naturreiche.* St. Petersburg: Gedruckt bey der Kayserl. Academie der Wissenschaften 1770–84. v.-. Illus.

> Library has volume 2.

141. Gogol, Nikolai V. *(Dead Souls) Chichikov's Journeys; or Home Life in Old Russia.* Translated by Bernard Guilbert Guerney,

introduction by Avrahm Yarmolinsky, and illustrated in color by Lucille Corcos. New York: Limited Editions Club, 1944. 2 v.; col. illus.

No. 434/1200. Signed by Lucille Corcos.

142. *Gosudarstvennaia Duma, stenograficheskie otchety* . . . [Parliament, Indices]. Ukazatel' k stenograficheskim otchetam . . . 1906. S.-Peterburg: 1907–.

143. *The Grand Duke Alexis in the United States of America.* With a new introduction by Jeff C. Dykes. New York: Interland Publishing, Inc. 1972. 221 pp.; illus.

Deluxe facsimile of 1872 American edition. No. 7/126. Signed by John M. Carroll, Jeff Dykes, and Joe Grandee.

144. Granovs'kyi, Alexander. *Peliustki nadii* [Flowers of Hope]. Kyiv: Vyd. I. Krements'koho, 1910. 126 pp.

145. Graves, Robert. *Ja, Klaudiusz* [I, Claudius]. Przełożył Stefan Essmanowski. Państwowy Instytut Wydawn., 1957. 588 pp.; diagram.

146. Graves, Robert. *Klaudiusz i Mesalina* [Claudius the God]. Przełożył Stefan Essmanowski. Warszawa: Państwowy Instytut Wydawn., 1958. 675 pp.

Grinevich, P.F. *See* Iakubovich, Petr F.

147. Grove, Florence C. *The Frosty Caucasus*: An Account of a Walk Through Part of the Range and of an Ascent of Elbruz in the Summer of 1874. With Illustrations Engraved by Ed. Whymper, From Photographs Taken During the Journey by H. Walker and a Map of the Country Traversed. London: Longmans, Green, 1875. ix, 341 pp.; illus., map.

Some Western authors who have been
published in Eastern Europe.

148. Gumilev, Nikolai S. *Shatior; stikhi* [Tent: Poems]. Revel':
Bibliofil, 1921. 52 pp.; illus.

149. Gurko, Vladimir I. *Tsar' i tsaritsa* [Tsar and Tsarina]. Paris:
Vozrozhdenie, 1927. 123 pp.

150. Hájek, Václav. *Kronyka czeska* [Czech Chronicle]. Vydal Jan
Ferdynand z Ssenfeldu. Praha: 1819. 264, 263 pp.; illus.
 Facsimile of the first edition dated 1541.

151. *Haliczanin* [The Galician]. Wydawany przez Walentego Chle-
dowskiego. We Lwowie: Drukiem Piotra Pillera, 1830–. v.-.
 Library has volumes 1 and 2.

152. Hanway, Jonas. *An Historical Account of the British Trade Over
the Caspian Sea:* With a Journal of Travels from London through
Russia into Persia; and back again through Russia, Germany, and
Holland. To which are added, the revolutions of Persia during
the present century, with the particular history of the great usurper
Nadir Kouli. London: Dodsley [*et al.*], 1753. 4 v. in 3; illus., maps.

153. Harkavy, Alexander. *A Contribution to Comparative Philology
Being Two Dissertations: 1. On the Russian Language. 2. On the Judaeo-
German Dialect.* New York: A. Ginsberg, 1892. Varying pagination.

154. Hasenko, Iurii. *Naiia iz dzhunglei; rasskazy* [Naiia]. Avtori-
zovannyi perevod s Ukrainskago Glieba Aleksiieva. Berlin: Izd.
O. D'iakovoi, 1922. 69 pp.; illus.

155. Hnatiuk, Volodymyr. *Das Geschlechtleben des ukrainischen
Bauernvolkes.* Folklorische Erhebungen. Leipzig: Deutsche Verlag-
aktiengesellschaft, 1909–1912. 2 v.; illus.
 "Privatdruck. Nur für Gelehrte. . . ." Zahl 199.

30

156. Höfler, Karl A. *Geschichtschreiber der husitischen Bewegung in Böhmen.* Wien: Hof-und Staatsdruckerei, 1856–66. 3 v.

157. Hofmann, Modeste. *Pushkin; pervaia glava nauki o Pushkine* [Pushkin]. Izd. 2. dop. Peterburg: Atenei, 1922. 196 pp.

158. Hofmann, Modeste. *Kniga o russkikh poetakh posledniago desiatilietiia* [Russian Poets of the Last Decade]. S.-Peterburg: Izd. T-va. M. Vol'f, 1907. 410 pp.; illus.

159. Hollo, Anselm. *Red Cats, English Versions.* San Francisco: City Lights Books, 1962. 64 pp.

    Twenty-five poems by Yevgeni Yevtushenko, Semyon Kirsanov, and Andrei Voznesensky. Translated by Anselm Hollo for Lawrence Ferlinghetti. Signed by the translator.

160. Houghton, Louise S. *The Russian Grandmother's Wonder Tales.* Illustrated by W.T. Benda. New York: C. Scribner, 1919. xvii, 347 pp.; illus.

161. Hus, Jan. *Dwanaczti czlankuo wijry křestianskee obeczné Dessýtí božých przikázanij a modlitby Páňe Otče náss etč. wykladowé, každému spassenij žádagiczýmu krzesttianu náypotrzebňéyssij* [Twelve Parts of the Christian Faith]. Praha: 1927. Unpaginated; illus.

    Facsimile of edition printed in 1520, W Praze: M. Konač.

162. Iakubovich, Petr F. *Ocherki russkoi poezii* [Commentaries on Russian Poetry]. S.-Peterburg: Izd. red. zhurnala "Russkoe bogatsvo", 1911. 403 pp.

Igor Tale. *See* Slovo o polku Igorevie.

163. Ioann, Bp. of San Francisco. *Prorocheskii dukh v russkoi poezii; (lirika Alekseia Tolstogo)* [The Prophetic Spirit in Russian Poetry;

Aleksei Tolstoi's Lyric Poetry]. Berlin: Izd-vo Za tserkov', 1938. 41 pp.

164. Ivanov, Georgii V. *Raspad atoma* [The Splitting of an Atom]. Paris: Maison du Livre Etranger, 1938. 86 pp.

165. *Izborniki Sviatoslava of 1073 and 1076.*

   A general title applied to miscellanies of didactic, gnomic, spiritual, ecclesiastic, and moralistic writings.

   There were two codices compiled by "Ioan the Scribe" in 1073 and 1076 for Sviatoslav, the Grand Prince of Kiev. The full text of the Izbornik of 1073 is known in many later copies. At least two Greek manuscripts are known whose contents correspond to the Izbornik of 1073 nearly word for word. The Izbornik of 1076, on the other hand, is not known in a complete copy; it is less dependent on Greek models and is the more interesting of the two.

   The Izbornik of 1076 was used to evaluate the original literary style of Kievan Rus' and especially to describe the autochtonous elements in Kievan social and political thought.

   The Izborniki are the second and the third oldest manuscripts that have come from the Eastern Slavic area.

165a. *Izbornik Sviatoslava 1073 goda* [Sviatoslav's Collection of the Year 1073]. Redkollegiia B. Rybakov *et al.* Khud. A. Serebriakov. Faks. izd. Moskva: Kniga, 1983. 2 v.; illus., facsims. V. 1: Nauchnyi aparat faksim. izd. V. 2: Faksim. izd.

165b. *Izbornik Sviatoslava 1076 goda* [Sviatoslav's Collection of the Year 1076]. Redkollegiia B. Rybakov *et al.* Khud. A. Serebriakov. Faks. izd. Moskva: Kniga, 1983. 2 v.; illus., facsims. V. 1: Nauchnyi aparat faksim. izd. V. 2: Faksim. izd.

166. Iziumov, Ovsii P. *Pravopysnyi slovnyk* [Orthographic Dictionary]. Kharkiv: Rad. shkola, 1931. 580 pp.

167. Jakobson, Roman. *Noveishaia russkaia poeziia* [The Newest Russian Poetry]. Nabrosok 1. V Prage: "Politika", 1921. 68 pp.

168. James, John T. *Journal of a Tour in Germany, Sweden, Russia, Poland in 1813–14.* Third edition. London: J. Murray, 1819. 2 v.; illus.

169. Jones, Stephen. *The History of Poland:* From Its Origin as a Nation to the Commencement of the Year 1795. To Which is Prefixed An Accurate Account of the Geography and Government of That Country and the Customs and Manners of Its Inhabitants. Dublin: Printed by William Porter for P. Wogan, [*et al.*] 1795. vii, 500 pp.; map.

170. Jordan, Max. *Das Königthum Georg's von Podebrad.* Leipzig: 1861. 535 pp.

171. *Kalevala; izbrannye runy* [Selected Runes From the Kalevala]. Red. K.F. Vediukova, illus. Tamary Iufa. Petrozavodsk: Karel'skoe knizhnoe izd-vo, 1967. 241 pp.; col. illus.

> Handwritten in ink on the verso of title page: "Having come to think of Eugene M. Kayden as a dear friend it is with affectionate regards that Sally and Rockwell Kent inscribe this little book to him —
>
> Rockwell Kent
> October 1967"

172. Kandinsky, Wassily. *Kandinsky; das graphische Werk* von Hans Konrad Roethel. Köln: M. DuMont Schauberg, 1970. xxix, 504 pp.; illus. (some col.).

173. Kandyba, Oleh. *Rin'* [Gravel]. Nakl. Bohdana Kravtseva, L'viv: 1935. 43 pp.

> Author's literary pseudonym, Oleh Olzhych, appears at head of title.

174. Karabchevskii, Nikolai P. *Chto glaza moi vidieli* [What My Eyes Have Seen]. V Berline: Izdanie O. D'iakovoi, 1921. 168 pp.; 2 v. in 1.

175. Karłowicz, Jan. *Słownik gwar polskich* [Dictionary of Polish Dialects]. Kraków: Nakł. Akademii Umiejętności, 1900–11. 6 v. in 3.

176. Karnovich, Evgenii P. *Zamiechatel'nyia bogatstva chastnykh lits v Rossii* [The Remarkable Wealth of Some Individuals in Russia]. 2. ispr. i dop. izd. S.-Peterburg: Izd. A.S. Suvorina, 1885. 330 pp.

177. Khodasevich, Vladislav F. *Derzhavin*. Parizh: Sovremennyia zapiski, 1931. 313 pp.; illus.

178. Khodasevich, Vladislav F. *Sobranie stikhov* [Collected Poems]. Paris: Vozrozhdenie, 1927. 183 pp.

179. Khomiakov, Aleksei S. *Izbrannyia stikhotvoreniia* [Selected Poems]. Petrograd: Izd. Akts. obshch. t-va tip. Diela, 1915. 64 pp.; illus.

180. Kisch, Cecil H. *The Waggon of Life, and Other Lyrics by Russian Poets of the Nineteenth Century*. Foreword by C.M. Bowra. London: Cresset Press, 1947. xv, 77 pp.
    No. 340/1500.

181. Kizevetter, Aleksandr A. *Istoricheskie ocherki* [Historical Sketches]. Moskva: A.A. Levenson, 1912. 542 pp.

182. Kliuchevskii, Vasilii O. *Skazaniia inostrantsev o Moskovskom gosudarstvie* [The Moscovite State as Described by Foreigners].

Petrograd: Lit-izd. Otdel Komissariata Narodnogo Prosveshcheniia, 1918. 333 pp.

183. *Kniga kratkikh pouchenii o glavneishikh spasitel'nikh dogmatakh very, i zapovedekh Bozhiikh, i o dolzhnostiakh, iz raznykh sviatykh otets i uchitelei sobrannaia* [Teachings on Christian Dogma]. Moskva: 1795. 263 pp.

184. Kollár, Jan. *Rozprawy o gmenách, počátkách i Starožitnostech národu Slawského a jeho kmenů* [Discourses on the Settlements, Origins and Antiquity of the Slavs]. W Budjne. W Králo universické tiskárné, 1830.

185. Kol'tsov, Aleksei V. *Stikhotvoreniia* [Poems]. S portretom avtora, ego faksimile i stat'eiu o ego zhizni i sochineniiakh, pisannoiu V. Bielinskim. Izd. K. Soldatenkova and N. Shepkina Moskva: V tip. Aleksandra Semena, 1856. 248, vi pp.; illus.

186. Kon, Feliks I. *Sorok let pod znamenem revoliutsii* [Forty Years Under the Revolutionary Banner]. Moskva-Petrograd: Gos izd-vo, [192–?]. 146 pp.

187. Kondakov, Nikodim P. *The Russian Icon*. Prague: Seminarium Kondakovianum, 1928–33. 4 v. in 3; illus., (some col.).

188. *Königinhof Manuscript.* Polyglotta Kralodvorského rukopisu, text v póvodnim i ovnoveném pravopisu; preklad: ruský, srbský, illyrský, polský, hornolužický, vlaský, anglický, nemecký: ukázky: dolnolužickego, maloruského, krajnského, francouzského i bolgarského. Vyd. Váceslava Hanky. V Praze: Nakl. vydavatelovým, 1852. x, 806 pp.; illus.

> A modern forgery of a Czech manuscript perpetrated by V. Hanka, J. Linda, and V.N. Svoboda.

189. Kopta, Josef. *Modrý námořník* [Blue Sailor]. Dobrodružná trilogie. l. vyd. V Praze: Melantrich, 1947. 451 pp.; illus. (some col.).

190. Kościuszko, Tadeusz. *Kosciuszko au peuple francais.* Paris: Pougin, 1796. Varying pagination; illus.

191. Kostomarov, Nikolai I. *Pis'mo N.I. Kostomarova k izdateliu "Kolokola"* [A Letter by Kostomarov to the Publisher of "The Bell"]. S predisloviem M. Dragomanova, Izd. "Gromady". Zheneva: Tip. "Gromady", 1885. ix, 13 pp.

192. Kotliarevs'kyi, Ivan. *Eneida na ukrains'ku movu perelytsiovana* [Aeneid]. Berlin: O. Diakova, 1922. 106 pp.; illus.

193. Kotoshikhin, Grigorii K. *O Rossii v tsarstvovanie Aleksiia Mikhailovicha; sovremennoe sochinenie* [Russia in the Reign of Tsar Alexis Mikhailovich]. Izd. 3. S.-Peterburg: Izd. Arkheograficheskoi kommissii 1884. xxxvi, 196, xx pp.; illus.

194. Kovalenko, Oleksa. *Ternovyi vinok; literaturno artystychnyi al'manakh* [Crown of Thorns]. Maliunky Buriachka, Slastiona, Hnidasha . . . Kyiv: Vyd. Iv. Samonenka, 1908. 191, 12 pp.; illus., (some col.).
   This artistic and literary almanac features the poetry, prose and drama of 44 authors and 12 painters.

Kralodvorsky, rukopis.   *See* Königinhof Manuscript.

195. Kraszewski, Jósef. *Stara baśń powieść dziewiątego wieku* [Ancient Tale]. Illustrated by E.M. Androlli. Wyd. jubileuszowe z portretem autora. Warszawa: Nakład Gebethnera i Wolffa, 1879. 432 pp.; illus.

Title page, *Ternovyi vinok*
by O. Kovalenko. (No. 194)

196. Križanić, Juraj. *Russkoe gosudarstvo v polovine XVII vieka; rukopis' vremen tsaria Alekseia Mikhailovicha* [The Russian State in the Midst of the XVII Century]. Otkryl i izdal P. Bezsonov. Moskva: V Tip. A. Semena, 1859–60. 2 v.

197. Križanić, Juraj. *O promyslie* [On Trade]. Sochinnenie togo zhe avtora, kak i "Russkoe gosudarstvo v polovine XVII vieka." Sviedieniia ob otkrytoi rukopisi P. Bezsonova. Moskva: V Tip. A. Semena, 1860. 128 pp.

198. Krukovskii, Adrian V. *Vladimir Solov'ev, kak myslitel' i cheloviek* [Vladimir Solov'ev]. K piatilietiiu ego konchiny, 31-go iiulia, 1905g. Vil'na: Tip. "Russkii Pochin," 1905. 45 pp.

199. Krylov, Ivan A. *Basni* [Fables]. S.-Peterburg: V tip. A. Pokhorskago, 1819. 95 pp.

> This first collected edition of Krylov's fables contains 139 tales. Kayden's holographic note on the front end-paper tells us that the first edition of 1808 only contained 23 fables.

200. Krylov, Ivan A. *Basni* [Fables]. Moskva: Gos. izd-vo khudozh. lit-ry, 1947. 100 pp.; illus.

201. Krylov, Ivan A. *Fables russes.* Tirées du recueil de M. Krylof, et imitées en vers français, par divers auteurs; précédées d'une introduction. Publiées par J.B. Einerling. Ornées de quatre gravures. St. Pétersbourg: Chez l'éditeur dans sa propre maison, 1845. vi, 210 pp.; illus.

202. Kubiiovych, Volodymyr. *Atlias Ukrainy i sumezhnykh kraiv* [Atlas of Ukraine and Adjoining Countries]. Tekhn. opratsiuvannia kart previv M. Kul'chyts'kyi. L'viv: Ukr. vydavnychyi in-t, 1937. xlvii, 66 pp.; fold. col. maps, diagrs., tables.

203. Kulish, Panteleimon. *Hryhorii Kvitka (Osnov'ianenko) i ioho povisti; slovo na novyi vykhod Kvitchynykh povistei* [The Novels of Kvitka]. Sanktpeterburg: 1858. xxxvi pp.

Kvitka's works are the most important contribution of Ukrainian classicism to the treasury of that national ideology.

204. Kuzmin, Mikhail A. *Sieti* [Nets]. 1. kniga stikhov. Oblozhka raboty N. Feofillktova. Moskva: Skorpion, 1908. 222 pp.

On July 24, 1969, Eugene Kayden wrote to Henry Waltemade of the University Libraries: "[This book] is [a] first edition of [a] famous poet before [the] Revolution; [it is] "pure" poetry, disliked by [the] Soviets . . . his work not reprinted to this day." The book came from the Kayden home library.

205. Kuznetsov, Anatolii V. *Babi Yar.* A document in the form of a novel. Translated by David Floyd. London: Cape., 1970. 478 pp.; maps.

Author's autographed presentation copy.

206. *Kyivs'kyi derzhavnyi muzei rossiis'koho mystetstva; zhyvopys'* [Kiev State Museum of Russian Art]. Uporiadnyk i avtor peredmovy O.V. Malashenko. Kyiv: Derzh. vyd-vo obrazotvorchoho mystetstva i muzychnoi lit-ry URSR, 1962. xxxviii pp.; 95 col. plates (in portfolio).

207. Kyrylenko, Orest. *Ukraintsi v Amerytsi* [Ukrainians in America]. Viden': Nakladom Soiuza Vyzvolennia Ukrainy, 1916. 40 pp.

208. Lamanskii, Vladimir. *Secrets d'état de Venise: documents, extraits, notices, et études servant à éclaircir les rapports de la seigneurie avèc les Grècs, les Slaves, et la porte ottomane à la fin du XVe et au XVIe siécle.* Saint-Pétersbourg: L'academie imperiale des sciences, 1884. Varying pagination.

209. Lenin, Vladimir I. *The Teachings of Karl Marx.* New York: International Publishers, 1930. 48 pp.

210. Leont'ev, Konstantin N. *Sobranie sochinenii* [Collected Works]. Moskva: Izd. V.M. Sablina, 1912–13. 9 v.; illus.

211. Lermontov, Mikhail I. *The Circassian Boy.* Translated through the German from the Russian by S.S. Conant. Boston: J.R. Osgood, 1875. 87 pp.

212. Lermontov, Mikhail I. *The Demon, and Other Poems.* Translated by Eugene M. Kayden. Introduction by Maurice Bowra. Yellow Springs, Ohio: Antioch Press, 1965. xxvi, 107 pp.; illus.

213. Lermontov, Mikhail I. *Piesnia pro tsaria Ivana Vasil'evicha, molodogo oprichnika i udalogo kuptsa Kalashnikova.* Boiarin Orsha. Kaznacheisha [The Ballad of Tsar Ivan Vasil'evich]. Praga: Slavianskoe izd-vo, 1920. 89 pp.

214. Lermontov, Mikhail I. *Pesnia pro tsaria Ivana Vasil'evicha, molodogo oprichnika i udalogo kuptsa Kalashnikova* [The Ballad of Tsar Ivan Vasil'evich]. Risunki I. Bilibina. Moskva: Goslitizdat, 1943. 18, 2 pp.; illus.

215. Lessing, Doris M. *No Witchcraft for Sale: Stories and Short Novels.* Moscow: Foreign Languages Publishing House, 1956. xiv, 315 pp.

216. Levertov, Denise. *Chekhov on the West Heath.* First edition. Andes, N.Y.: Woolmer/Brotherson, 1977. 14 pp.
    No. 177/200. Numbered and signed by the author.

Illustration for "Potemkinsche
Dörfer" by L. Bakst. (No. 217)

217. Levinson, Andrei I. *Leon Bakst.* Deutsche Ausg. Berlin: E. Wasmuth, 1925. 233 pp.; illus. (some mounted and col.).

No. 20/250. *See also*: Bakst, L., No. 25.

218. Lezhnev, A. *Dva poeta: Geine, Tiutchev* [Two Poets: Heine, Tiutchev]. Moskva: Khudozhestvennaia literatura, 1934. 349 pp.

219. Lezhohubs'kyi, Teodozii. *De znaity pravdu?* [Where Is Truth to Be Found?]. Philadelphia: 1916. 173 pp.

220. Linde, Samuel B. *Słownik języka polskiego* [Dictionary of the Polish Language]. W Warszawie: W drukarni Piiarów, 1807–1814. 6 v.

221. *Litopys Chervonoi Kalyny* [Chronicle]. 1922–1939. v.-. Illus. Library has 3 volumes, 1932–1935.

An important popular science journal, devoted to Ukrainian military affairs and to a struggle for liberation.

222. Lomonosov, Mikhail V. *Izbrannyia sochineniia: stikhi i proza* [Selected works]. S.-Peterburg: Izd. Akts. o-va tip. Diela, 1913. 134, 2 pp.; illus.

223. Lord, Albert B. *Russian Folk Tales.* Illustrated by Teje Etchemendy. New York: Printed for the Members of the Limited Editions Club, 1970. xx, 196 pp.; illus. (some col.).

No. 12/1500. Signed by Teje Etchemendy.

224. Lukasevych, Klavdiia. *Malorossiiskiia skazki dlia dietei* [Ukrainian Children's Stories]. Po sbornikam Chubinskago, Danilevskago, Afanaseva, Rudchenko, diadi Pufa i dr. Izd. 2-e. Moskva: Izd. I.D. Sytina, 1909.

42

225. Lukomskii, Georgii K. *La vie et les moeurs en Russie de Piérre le Grand à Lénine.* Paris: Librairie Ernest Leroux, 1928. viii, 45 pp.; illus.

226. Lukomskii, Georgii K. *Pamiatniki starinnoi arkhitektury Rossii* [Monuments of Early Russian Architecture]. Izd. 2. perev. i dop. Petrograd: V tip. Khudozh. stroitel'stva, 1916. 393, xxvii pp.; illus.

227. Lukomskii, Georgii K. *Staryi Peterburg: progulki po starinnym kvartalam* [Old Saint Petersburg: Touring the Ancient Streets]. Izd. 2. Petrograd: Svobodnoe iskusstvo, [1917?]. 81 pp.; illus.

228. Lukoms'kyi, Vladyslav. *Malorossiiskii gerbovnik* [Ukrainian Heraldry]. Sanktpeterburg: Izd. Chernigovskogo dvorianstva, 1914. xxv, 213, 12 pp.; illus.

229. Lyall, Robert. *Travels in Russia, the Krimea, the Caucasus, and Georgia.* London: Printed for T. Cadell, [*et al.*], 1825. 2 v.; illus.

230. *M.M. Vinaver: Russkaia obshchestvennost' nachala XX vieka* [M.M. Vinaver: Russian Society during the first half of the Twentieth Century]. Sbornik statei P.N. Miliukova [*et al.*]. Parizh: 1937. 222 pp.; illus.

231. Maiakovskii, Vladimir V. *Kem byt'?* [Whom to Become?] Risunki A. Pakhomova. Moskva: Gos. izd-vo detskoi lit-ry, 1948. 24 pp.; illus.

232. Maikov, Apollon N. *Polnoe sobranie sochinenii* [Collected Works]. S kritiko-biograficheskim ocherkom. 9. ispr. i dop. izd. pod red. P.V. Bikova. S. Peterburg: A.F. Marks, 1914. 4 v. in 2; illus.

Frontispiece for V. Lukoms'kyi's
Malorossiiskii gerbovnik. (No. 228)

233. Manntaufel, Petr. *Tales of a Naturalist.* Moscow: Foreign Languages Publishing House, [193–?]. 150 pp.

234. Manstein, Christof H. *Memoirs of Russia, Historical, Political, and Military, from the Year MDCCXXVII, to MDCCXLIV.* A Period comprehending many remarkable Events. In Particular the Wars of Russia with Turkey and Sweden. . . . Translated from the Original Manuscript of General Manstein. . . . Never before published. . . . London: Printed for T. Becket and P.A. De Hondt, 1770. viii, 424, 8 pp.; illus.

235. Markov, Vladimir. *Stikhi* [Poems]. Frankfurt a/M: Ekho, 1947. 62 pp.

236. Marshak, Samuil I. *Babies of the Zoo.* Translated from Russian; drawings by E. Charushin. Moscow: Mejdunarodnaya Kniga, [192—?]. 24 pp.; col. illus.

237. Marshak, Samuil I. *Pudel'* [Poodle]. Risunki M. Mituricha. Moskva: Detskii mir, 1960. 12 pp.; col. illus.

238. Marshak, Samuil I. *Verses for Children.* Translated by Margaret Wettlin, illustrated by V.V. Lebedev. Moscow: Foreign Languages Publishing House, [n.d.]. 48 pp.

239. Marshak, Samuil I. *A Whiskered Little Frisker.* Translated by E. Felgenhauer; drawings by V.V. Lebedev. Moscow: Foreign Languages Publishing House, [n.d.]. 14 pp.

240. Marvin, Charles. *Reconnoitering Central Asia:* Pioneering Adventures in the Region Lying Between Russia and India. London: W. Swan Sonnenschein, 1884. 421 pp.; illus.

241. Masaryk, Tomáš G. *The Making of a State. Memories and Observations, 1914–1918.* An English version, arranged and prepared with an introduction by Henry Wickham Steed. London: G. Allen & Unwin, 1927. 461 pp.; illus.

> This volume was presented to the University by Frank C. Lee. An autograph inscription on the half-title page reads: "As collaborator of President Masaryk, I sign Dr. Eduard Beneš. Praha, 28.1. 1935."

242. Maude, Aylmer. *Tolstoy on Art and Its Critics.* London (etc.): H. Milford, Oxford University Press, 1925. 30 pp.

243. Meilakh, Boris S. *A.S. Pushkin; ocherk zhizni i tvorchestva* [A.S. Pushkin, His Life and Literary Work]. Moskva: Izd-vo Akademii Nauk SSSR, 1949. 197 pp.; illus.

244. Mendeleev, Dmitrii. *K poznaniiu Rossii* [Learning About Russia]. S prilozheniem karty Rossii. S. Peterburg: Tipo-lit. M.P. Frolovoi, 1906. Varying pagination.

245. Mendelsohn. Shlama. *The Polish Jews Behind the Nazi Ghetto Walls.* New York: Yiddish Scientific Institute (YIVO), 1942. 31 pp.; illus.

246. Merezhkovskii, Dmitrii S. *Bylo i budet; dnevnik, 1910–1914* [Diary, 1910–1914]. Petrograd: 1915. 334 pp.

247. Merezhkovskii, Dmitrii S. *Griadushchii ham. Chekhov i Gor'kii* [The Coming Ham]. S.-Peterburg: Izd. M.V. Pirozhkova, 1906. 185 pp.

> Also includes author's: *Teper' ili nikogda. Strashnyi sud nad russkoi intelligentsiei. Sv. Sofiia. O novom religioznom dieistvii.*

248. Merezhkovskii, Dmitrii S. *L. Tolstoi i Dostoevskii* [Tolstoi and Dostoevskii]. 4. izd. S.-Peterburg: Obshchestvennaia Pol'za, 1903–1909. 2 v.

249. Merezhkovskii, Dmitrii S. *Prorok russkoi revolutsii; k iubileiu Dostoevskago* [Prophet of the Russian Revolution]. S.-Peterburg: Izd. M.V. Pirozhkova, 1906. 152 pp.

250. Merezhkovskii, Dmitrii S. *Sobranie stikhov, 1883–1903* [Collected Poems, 1883–1903]. Moskva: Skorpion, 1904. 182 pp.

251. Merezhkovskii, Dmitrii S. *Viechnye sputniki: Pushkin* [Eternal Companions: Pushkin]. 3 izd. S.-Peterburg: Pub. M.V. Pirozhkova, 1906. 90 pp.
    Part of the 1897 edition of *Viechnye sputniki, portrety iz vsemirnoi literatury.*

252. Metlyns'kyi, Amvrozii. *Tvory Amvroziia Metlyns'koho i Mykoly Kostomarova* [Works]. U L'vovi: Pros'vita, 1906. 493 pp.; illus.

253. Mijatovich, Elodie L. *Serbian Fairy Tales.* Illustrated by Sidney Stanley. London: William Heinemann, 1917. 204 pp.

254. Mikhailov, Sergei. *Rabbit Nose-in-the-Air.* A Fairy-Tale in Two Acts and a Prologue. Translated by I. Zheleznova; drawings by E. Rachev. Moscow: Foreign Languages Publishing House, 1962. 62, 2 pp.; illus.

255. Miklosich, Frantz. *Etymologisches Wörterbuch der slavischen Sprachen.* Wien: W. Braumüller, 1886. vii, 547 pp.

256. Miklosich, Frantz. *Dictionnaire abrégé de six langues slaves (russe, vieux-slave, bulgare, serbe, tchéque et polonaise) ainsi que français*

Illustration by S. Stanley for "Papalluga" from
E.L. Mijatovich's *Serbian Fairy Tales.* (No. 253)

et allemand, rédigé sous les auspices de Pierre d'Oldenbourg. St. Pétersbourg: M.O. Wolff, 1885. 955 pp.

257. Millay, Edna S. *The Murder of Lidice.* New York and London: Harper, 1942. vi, 32 pp.

A narrative poem.

258. *Missale Pragense z roku 1479* [Missal]. Praha: [1931?]. Facsimile edition. 522 pp.

259. Modzalevskii, Boris. *Pushkin pod tainym nadzorom* [Police Surveillance of Pushkin]. Sanktpeterburg: PARFENON, 1922. 56 pp.

260. Monahan, Barbara. *A Dictionary of Russian Gesture.* Ann Arbor, MI.: Hermitage, 1983. 184 pp.; illus.

261. *Moskovskii Malyi teatr, 1824–1924* [Moscow Little Theater]. Moskva: Gos. izd-vo, 1924. 707 pp.; illus.

Added to title page: Le Pétit théâtre de Muscow.

262. Mücke, Karl E. *Słownik dolnoserbskeje rěcy a jeje narečow* [Dictionary of the Sorbian Language and Its Dialects]. Praha: Nakl. Česke akademie věd a umeni, 1926–28. 3 v.

263. Musatov, Aleksei. *Stozhari Village; a Story.* Translated by R. Dickson; illustrated by O. Korovin. Moscow: Foreign Languages Publishing House, 1954. 232 pp.

Winner of the 1949 Stalin Prize for Soviet literature for young people, this book portrays life in the typical Soviet village during the last year of World War II.

264. Nabokov, Vladimir V. *Lolita.* Paris: Olympia Press, 1955. 2 v.

265. Nabokov, Vladimir V. *Pnin.* First edition. Garden City, New York: Doubleday, 1957. 191 pp.

266. Nabokov, Vladimir V. *Sogliadatai* [The Eye]. Paris: Izd-vo "Russkiia zapiski", 1938. 252 pp.

267. Nadson, Semen I. *Stikhi* [Poetry]. Berlin: Mysl', 1921. 62 pp.

268. Negedly, Johann. *Boehmische Grammatik.* Mit Tabellen und einem Anhange nach Meidingers Lehrart für Deutsche bearbeitet. Prag: In Commission in der Widtmann'schen Buchhandlung, 1804. 367 pp.

269. Nekrasov, Nikolai A. *Neizdannye stikhotvoreniia, varianty i pis'ma* [Unpublished Poems, Variants and Letters]. Iz rukopisnykh sobranii Pushkinskago doma pri Rossiiskoi akademii nauk. Petrograd: Izd-vo M. and S. Sabannikovikh, 1922. 303 pp.; illus.

270. Nekrasov, Nikolai A. *Moroz krasnyi - nos* [Red-Nose Frost]. Translated in the original meters from the Russian of N.A. Nekrasov with three illustrations designed and engraved by W.J. Linton. Second edition. Boston: Ticknor, 1887. 173 pp.; illus.

271. Nemcova, Božena. *The Disobedient Kids and Other Czechoslovak Fairy Tales.* Interpreted by William H. Tolman and V. Smetanka. Stories selected by V. Tille and illustrated by Artuš Scheiner. Prague: B. Koči, 1921. 46 pp.; illus. (some col.).

272. Neruda, Jan. *Letni vzpominký* [Summer Memories]. Malostansky feuilleton. [Praha?]: [193–]. Unpaginated; col. illus.

273. Nezval, Vitězslav. *Z domoviny* [From the Homeland]. 2. vyd. Praha: Československý spisovatel, 1958. 80 pp.

A surrealist poetic work which emphasizes connections between romantic and "dream-like qualities."

274. Niemcewicz, Julian. *Śpiewy historyczne z muzyką, rycinami i krótkim dodatkiem zbioru historyi polskiej* [Historic Songs]. Wyd. 5. Lwów: Nakładem K. Jabłońskiego, 1849. xvi, 320 pp.; illus.

275. *Nikolai II. Materialy dlia kharakterisitiki lichnosti i tsarstvovaniia* [Nicholas II. A Study of His Personality and of His Reign]. Red. S.P. Mel'gunov. Moskva: Izd. Zhurnala "Golos minuvshago", 1917. 255 pp.

276. Nikolai Nikolaevich, Grand Duke of Russia. *Imperator Aleksandr I, opyt istoricheskago issliedovaniia* [Emperor Alexander I]. S.-Peterburg: 1912. 2 v.; illus. (some col.).

277. Nikol'skii, Vladimir V. *Idealy Pushkina;* aktovaia rech' V.V. Nikol'skago. S prilozheniem statei togo zhe avtora "Zhober i Pushen" i "Dantes-Genoren" [Pushkin's Ideals]. Izd. 4. ispr. i dop. zamietkoiu togozhe avtora "K bibliografii Evgeniia Onegina." S.-Peterburg: Tip. A.S. Suvorina, 1899. x, 152 pp.
    Author's autographed presentation copy.

278. Nyka, Josef. *Ostatni atak na Kunyang Chhish* [The Final Attack on the Hindu Kush]. Opracowanie: Josef Nyka, Andrzej Paczkowski, Andrzej Zawada. Warszawa: Wydawnictwo Sport i Turystyka, 1973. 255, 3 pp.; illus., maps.

279. *Obrazne slovo: postiini narodni porivniannia* [The Figurative Word]. Zibrav i uporiadkuvav Ivan Huryn. Kyiv: Dnipro, 1974. 237 pp.; illus.

Olzhych, Oleh. *See* Kandyba, Oleh.

ИДЕАЛЫ

ПУШКИНА

Inscription on half-title page by V.V.
Nikol'skii for *Idealy Pushkina*. (No. 277)

280. Onasch, Konrad. *Ikonen.* [Gütersloh]: Gotersloher Verlagshaus, 1961. 431 pp.; col. illus.

281. Orwell, George. *Kolhosp tvaryn; kazka* [Animal Farm]. Z anhliis'koi movy pereklav Ivan Cherniatyns'kyi. [Munich]: Prometei, [194–]. 90 pp.; illus.

> Orwell wrote a special preface for the Ukrainian edition of this satire on dictatorship in English. It was lost and has been re-cast into English from the Ukrainian. An organization of Ukrainian displaced persons distributed the book in Munich in November 1947.

282. *Otechnik* [Patericon]. Paterik Pecherskii, snest'. [Kiev]: Kievopecherskaia Lavra, 1820. Varying pagination.

283. Palacký, František *Documenta Mag. Johannis Hus. vitam, doctrinam, causam in constantiensi concilio actam, et controversias de religione in Bohemia annis 1403–1418 motas illustrantia, quae partim adhuc inedita, partim mendose vulgata, nunc ex ipsis fontibus hausta. . . .* Pragae: Fridericus Tempsky, 1869. xv, 768 pp.

284. Palacký, František. *Literarische Reise nach Italien im Jahre 1837 zur Aufsuchung von Quellen der bömishen und mährischen Geschichte.* Prag: Kronberger's Witwe und Weber, 1838. 122 pp.

285. Palacký, František. *Radhost; sbírka spisůw drobných z oboru řeči a literatury české, krasówědy, historie a politiky* [Happiness; A Collection of Essays and Speeches on Czech Literature, Science of Art, History and Politics]. W Praze: Nákl. B. Tempského, 1871–73. 3 v. in 1.

286. Palacký, František. *Urkundliche Beiträge zur Geschichte Böhmens und seiner Nachbarländer im Zeitalter Georg's von Podierbrad*

(1450–1471). Wien: Kaiserlich Königliche Hof- und Staatsdruckerei, 1860. 2 v.

> Library has volume 1.

287. Palacký, František. *Urkundliche Beiträge zur Geschichte des Hussitenkrieges.* Prag: Friedrich Tempsky, 1873. 2 v.

288. *Palekh; isskusstvo sovetskogo Palekha* [The Art of Soviet Palekh]. Moskva: Sovetskii khudozhnik, 1958. 54 pp.; illus. (some col.).

289. Pallas, Peter S. *Voyages du professeur Pallas, dans plusieurs provinces de l'empire de Russie et dans l'Asie septentrionale; tr. de l'allemand par le c. Gauthier de la Peyronie.* Nouv. éd., rév. et enrichie de notes par les cc. Lamarch . . . et Langles. . . . Paris: Maradan, l'an II de la Republique, 1794. 9 v.

290. *Pamiati pogibshikh; sbornik* [A Collection in Memory of the Dead]. Pod red. N.I. Astrova [*et al.*]. Parizh: 1929. 231 pp.; illlus.

291. *Pamięci Wilhelma Feldmana* [In Memory of Wilhelm Feldman]. Jan Baudouin de Courtenay *et al.* List otwarty Wilhelma Feldmana do Fryderyka Naumanna. Kraków: Drukarnia narodowa, 1922. 204 pp.; illus.

292. Partyts'kyi, Omelian. *Hramatyka iazyka ruskoho dlia uzhytku v shkolakh liudovykh* [Ukrainian Grammar]. L'viv: Pechatano v pechatni Stavropyhiiskoho Instytuta, 1871. 142 pp.

> One of the first works on linguistics in Galicia (Western Ukraine).
> The original title page is missing.

Palekh illustration on a casket, 1934, in the State Museum of
Palekh Art. "Tale of Tsar Saltan" by A.V. Kotukhin. (No. 288)

293. *Passional, čili, Život a umučení všech sviatých mučedlníkův* [The Life and Death of All the Holy Martyrs]. V Praze: 1926. Unpaginated; illus.

Facsimile of 1495 edition.

294. Pasternak, Boris L. Correspondence to Eugene M. Kayden, July 1958 to December 1959. Kayden's replies are in the Pasternak archives in Moscow.

Two postcards written on both sides in a clear hand in English and signed. Typed transcriptions made by Kayden. Pasternak thanks Kayden profusely: "I could not prevent my tears to run down at the acknowledgment of Pushkin lines and tenors through the animated and sonorous English sounding . . . they must be very good. . . ." Pasternak explains that he writes in English for "consideration of safety."

Three letters (10 pages total) with their envelopes, all holographic, signed, and in English. Typed transcriptions made and signed by Kayden, each with a commentary. Towards the end of his life (Pasternak died on May 30, 1960) Pasternak notes that he writes fewer letters because of his "experiences and trials." He feels it is better not to reveal his true feelings. Later, Kayden notes, Pasternak admitted he had a heart ailment, but "outsiders did not know about his serious illness." In a letter to the University of Colorado Librarian dated June 13, 1968, Kayden explains that the "Letter of August 22, by airmail registered, is especially valuable" because Pasternak makes a clear statement of his poetic philosophy. Kayden quotes this statement in the introduction of his second edition of Pasternak's poems (No. 299).

295. Pasternak, Boris L. *The Christmas Pine Tree*. Translated by Eugene M. Kayden. Kansas City, Mo.: Hallmark, [n.d.]. Greeting card.

Contains holographic greeting: "To Sima with my love, Eugene."

296. Pasternak, Boris L. *The Collected Prose Works*. Introduction by Stefan Schimanski. London: L. Drummond Ltd. 1945. 213, 1 pp.; illus.

Heavily annotated and marked by Eugene M. Kayden.

297. Pasternak, Boris L. *Kogda razguliaetsia* [When the Skies Clear]. [n.p.], [n.d.]. Unpaginated (53 pp.) set of poems in hectograph copy.

> Eugene Kayden's holographic note with the poems is as follows: "Boris Pasternak. Kogda Razguliayetsa. (When the Skies Clear) 1955–1959 44 poems. *Two Parts Part I*: 34 Poems dated 1955–58 (eight appeared in *Znamia*, September 1956). Supplement: 10 poems dated 1956–59. Variant readings given in footnotes. Texts were circulating secretly in USSR. *One* set reached friends of Pasternak in Germany (Munich?) and few hectograph copies made. *Two* were mailed to U.S., one to Professor Gleb Struve [of the University of California], and one to me. I received my set from Victor S. Frank. Mr. Frank supervised the hectograph process. —EM Kayden"

298. Pasternak, Boris L. *Poems.* Translated by Eugene M. Kayden. Ann Arbor: University of Michigan Press, 1959. 194 pp.; illus.

> "To University of Colorado Library. From Boris Pasternak and his translator. Eugene Kayden, B.A. 1912"

299. Pasternak, Boris L. *Poems.* Translated by Eugene M. Kayden. Second edition. Revised and enlarged. Yellow Springs, Ohio: Antioch Press, 1964. xxiv, 312 pp.; illus.

> "To my great undergraduate teachers -1908–1912- Hellems, Norlin and Libby. In memoriam Eugene Kayden, Christmas 1968".

300. Pasternak, Boris L. *The Poems of Doctor Zhivago.* Translated by Eugene M. Kayden; drawings by Bill Greer. Kansas City, Mo.: Hallmark Editions, 1967. 61 pp.; col. illus.

> Translator's autographed presentation copy.

301. Pasternak, Boris L. *The Poems of Doctor Zhivago.* Translated by Eugene M. Kayden with an introduction by James Morgan. Illustrated by Bill Greer. Kansas City, Mo.: Hallmark Crown Editions, 1971. 69 pp.; col. illus.

In a note to the University of Colorado Libraries, Kayden wrote: "May Pasternak's vision of life and social holiness be your inspiration in living your own life."

Kayden also inserted and pasted a typed note into the gift copy: "Books often become valuable, special, even rare, expensive collectors' items, by virtue of some misprint. My translation of Pasternak's THE POEMS OF DOCTOR ZHIVAGO is blessed with a number of misprints, here indicated on pp. 41, 50, 56, 66. There is also one great blunder on p. 10 where the author of the Introduction, James Morgan, speaks of Dr. Zhivago of having noticed his Lara from the window of the street car, forces his way out, only to fall dead on the pavement from a heart attack. . . . He did not see Lara. She wasn't there. (Read the book! That one "small" error in a translation has destroyed the spiritual symbolism of the whole novel. Poor Pasternak!)

Cordially yours,

[signed]

Eugene M. Kayden
Class of 1912, B.A."

Kayden has corrected the typos on the above mentioned pages with black ink.

302. Pasternak, Boris L. *Poetry, 1914–1960.* Selected, edited, and translated by George Reavey. New York: Putnam's Capricorn Books, 1960. 257 pp.

303. Pasternak, Boris L. Portraits. Two photographs, one glossy and one matte-finish, sent to Eugene Kayden in envelope. Both have holographic inscriptions on back: "A gift from Boris Pasternak, Feb. 1959" to Eugene M. Kayden.

304. Pasternak, Boris L. *Sestra moia zhizn'; leto 1917 goda* [My Sister Life; Summer of 1917]. Berlin: Izd-vo Z.I. Grzhebina, 1923. 115 pp.; illus.

БОРИС ПАСТЕРНАК

СЕСТРА МОЯ ЖИЗНЬ

Лето 1917 года

ИЗДАТЕЛЬСТВО З. И. ГРЖЕБИНА
БЕРЛИН / ПЕТЕРБУРГ   МОСКВА
1923

Title page and portrait drawing by I. Annenkov for B. Pasternak's *Sestra moia zhizn'*. (No. 304)

305. Pasternak, Boris L.   From *Snows Are Falling*. Translated by Eugene M. Kayden. Kansas City, Mo.: Hallmark, 1960. Greeting card.

306. Pasternak, Boris L.   *Star of the Nativity*. Translated by Eugene M. Kayden. Kansas City, Mo.: Hallmark, 1959. Greeting card.

307. Pasternak, Boris L.   *Stikhotvoreniia Iuriia Zhivago*. Chast' semnadtsataia [Poems by Iurii Zhivago. Part Seventeen]. 41 pp.

> In a letter dated June 13, 1968, to Henry Waltemade, Special Collections, Norlin Library, Eugene Kayden wrote: "Since you already have my three books of Pasternak translations, I want the Norlin Library to have other material. . . . Thermofax of POEMS OF DOCTOR ZHIVAGO, of Pasternak's Russian typewritten copy, forming pages 393–433 of the novel. Poems are numbered 1 - 25 at end of novel. There are minute corrections on pp. 397, 406, 407, 408. I have assumed that Pasternak has instructed the Italian publisher, G. Feltrinelli, or his agent, to send a thermofax copy for my use as translator."

308. Pasternak, Boris L.   *Stikhotvoreniia v odnom tome* [Poems in One Volume]. Otv. redaktor N. Tikhonov. Leningrad: Izd-vo pisatelei v Leningrade, 1933. 429 pp.; illus.

> On verso of portrait frontispiece in Eugene Kayden's handwriting: "Boris Pasternak painted by A. Yar-Kravchenko, 1933." On the title page, also in Kayden's hand: "Eugene M. Kayden A gift to me from Pasternak - 1940 December 25. *N.B.* Revised lines, shown here in ink, were supplied by Pasternak, based on unpublished editions of his poetry for 1957. —EMK."

309. Pelzel, Franz M.   *Kurzgefaszte Geschichte der Böhmen, von den ältesten bis auf die neuesten Zeiten*. Aus den besten Geschichteschreibern, alten Kroniken, und glaubwürdigen Handschriften zusammen getragen. 2. verm. verb. und fortgesetzte Aufl. Prag: Hagen, 1779. 2 v. in 1.

310. *Pervyia russkiaa viedomosti, pechatavshiiasia v Moskvie v 1703 godu* [First Russian Newspaper, Published in Moscow in 1703]. Novoe tisnenie po dvum ekzempliaram, khraniashchimsia v Imp. Publichnoi Bibliotekie. S.-Peterburg: 1855. 30, 262, 51 pp.

311. Petr z Rožmberka. *Pergkwerch Ordnung.* V Praze, 1930. Unpaginated.

> Facsimile edition of work published in 1515 in Vienna by Johann Winnterburger. "Petra z Rožmberga Horniřad z r. 1515, napsal Zdeněk V. Tobolka."

312. Petryts'kyi, Anatol'. *Teatral'ni stroi* [Stage Costumes]. Tekst Khmuroho. Kharkiv: Derzh. vyd-vo Ukrainy, 1929. 23 pp.; illus. (some col.).

> A Futurist artist at home in traditional as well as modern European techniques, Petryts'kyi's designs were a cornerstone in post-revolutionary Ukrainian theater.

313. *Piesné duchownie ewāgelittské, znowu přehlednuté, zprawené a shromážděné y také mnohé wnowe složné yrūtu a zakládu pisem swatých* [Protestant Hymns]. Ke cti a k chwále samého ydinéo wécného Boha w Troycy blažné. Také ku pomacy a k Službé y k potěssenj w prawém krestanském ńaboženstwj wssech wěrných miluyicých y národ y jazyk czeský. Praha, [1930?]. 1 v. Various pagination. At head of title: Piesně chural božskych.

> Facsimile edition of 1541 work published in Prague by Jan Rohač.

314. Pigarev, Kirill V. *Zhizn' i tvorchestvo Tiutcheva* [The Life and Work of Tiutchev]. Moskva: Izd-vo Akademii nauk SSSR, 1962. 373 pp.; illus.

315. Pinter, Harold. *The Tea Party.* Issued as "Gorgona 8, 1965." Zagreb: Josip Vanista, [1965?] Private edition. 5 pp.

> This short story, a precursor of the play with the same title, was first printed in *Playboy Magazine*, January 1965. The Zagreb text is

at variance with that in *Playboy*, probably due to an imperfect understanding of the English language.

316. *Pisni z polonyny: zakarpats'ki narodni pisni* [Songs From a Mountain Valley]. Zapysav i uporiadkuvav Petro Poida. 3 vyd. Kyiv: Dnipro, 1974. 238 pp.

317. Platonov, Sergei F. *Ivan Groznyi* [Ivan the Terrible]. Berlin: Obelisk, 1924. 134 pp.

318. Platonov, Sergei F. *Petr Velikii; lichnost' i deiatel'nost'* [Peter the Great: Man and Ruler]. Leningrad: Vremia, 1926. 113, 1 pp.

319. *Plody; sbornik literaturnikh proizvedenii* [Fruits; a Literary Anthology]. Pod red. Dona Mikli. Cambridge: 1952. 63 pp.; illus.
    A typed and mimeographed festschrift in Russian and English for Professor Elizabeth Fedorovna Hill. Includes short stories and poems. One of 50 copies produced by Russian literature students at Cambridge University, England, 1952.

320. *Pobezhdennye vershiny: sbornik sovetskogo al'pinizma, 1975–1978* [Conquered Heights: Soviet Mountaineering, 1975–1978]. Redkol. P.S. Rototaev [*et al*]. Moskva: Mysl', 1981. 278 pp.; illus., maps.

321. *A Pocket Guide to the Soviet Union.* Issued by INTOURIST (State Tourist Company, USSR). First edition. Moscow: Vneshtorgizdat, 1932. 706 pp.; maps.

322. *Poeziia revolutsionnoi Moskvy* [The Poetry of Revolutionary Moscow]. Pod red. I. Erenburga. Berlin: Mysl', 1922. 125 pp.

323. Polevoi, Petr N. *Russian Fairy Tales From the Skazki of Polevoi* by R. Nisbet Bain. Illustrated by C.M. Gere. New York: A.L. Burt, [189–?]. xv–vi, 304 pp.; illus.

324. Polevoi, Petr N. *Istoriia russkoi slovesnosti s drevneishikh vremen do nashykh dnei* [A History of Russian Linguistics From Ancient Times to the Present]. S.-Peterburg: Izd. A.F. Marksa, 1900. 3 v.; illus. (some col.).

325. Polievktov, Mikhail A. *Nikolai I; biografiia i obzor tsarstvovaniia* [A Biography and Review of the Reign of Nicholas I]. Moskva: Izd-vo M. i S. Sabashnikovykh, 1918. 392 pp.

326. *Polnyi sbornik platform vsiekh russkikh politicheskikh partii* [A Collection of the Platforms for All the Russian Political Parties]. S.-Peterburg: Izd. N.L. Nyrkina, 1907. 48 pp.

327. Polo, Marco. *The Travels of Marco Polo.* Revised and edited by Manuel Komroff. Illustrated by Nikolai F. Lapshin. New York: Limited Editions Club, 1934. 2 v.; col. illus.
    No. 1250/1500. Signed by N.F. Lapshin.

328. Polons'ka-Vasylenko, Nataliia. *Istoriko-kul'turnyi atlas po russkoi istorii s ob'iasnitel'nym tekstom* [Historico-Cultural Atlas of Russian History]. Pod red. M. V. Dovnar-Zapol'skago. Kiev: Izd. V.S. Kul'zhenko, [1912?–]. v.-. Illus.
    Library has volumes 2 and 3.

329. Pontanus, Georgius B. *Bohaemia pia, hoc est, historia brevis, pietatem avitam Bohemiae e miraculis, ducibus et regibus, sanctis quoque . . . et ex aliis ostendens, quinque libris comprehensa.* Accedunt insuper res quaedam gestae sub Ludovico rege hactenus non evulgata. Bound in Freher, Marquard: Rerum Bohemicarum. Francofurti, Claud. Marnius et heredes Io. Aubrii, 1608. Varying pagination.

330. Porter, Jane. *Thaddeus of Warsaw.* With a new introduction, notes, etc., by the author. New York: Thomas Y. Crowell, 1831. 517 pp.

331. *Poselstvi* [Embassies]. Číslo l-říj. Chicago: Czechoslovak National Council of America, [1917–]. v.-. Illus.

332. Postupal'skii, Igor' S. *Literaturnyi trud Davida Burliuka* [Literary Work of David Burliuk]. New York: M. Burliuk, 1931. 15 pp.; illus.

> Inscription by Burliuk on the front wrapper: "Sergeiu Iur'evichu Sudeiikinu v znak pamiati, s vozhedeleniem imet' kogda libo chto libo iz ego divnykh proizvedenii." [To Sergei Iu. Sudeikin, a symbol of rememberance, with lust to own one of his wonderful creations at some point.]
>
> A discussion of Burliuk's work and his influence on "proletarian futurism."

333. *Práwa mestska Králowstwj Czeského a Margkrabstwj morawskeho* [Bohemia and Moravia. Laws, Statutes]. W Brně: Wytisstěno u F.I. Synápj, 1701. 226 pp.; illus.

334. Priesniakov, Aleksandr E. *Moskovskoe tsarstvo* [Moscow Kingdom]. Petrograd: Ogni, 1918. 139 pp.

335. *Programmy kontsertov A.G. Rubinshteina s primiechaniiami i poiasneniiami.* Anton Rubinstein concert programs with notes and laid-in newspaper clippings. S.-Peterburg: Tip. R. Golike, 1886. 55 pp.; illus.

336. Prokof'ev, Sergei S. *Peter and the Wolf.* Illustrated by Warren Chappell. With a foreword by Serge Koussevitsky. New York: Alfred A. Knopf, 1940. Unpaginated.

337. Pushkin, Aleksandr S. *Bakhchisaraiskii fontan; sochinenie* [The Fountain of Bakhchisarai]. Moskva: V tip. A. Semena, 1824. 48 pp.; illus.

БАХЧИСАРАЙСКІЙ

ФОНТАНЪ.

Сочиненіе

АЛЕКСАНДРА ПУШКИНА.

Многіе, шакже какъ и я, посѣщали
сей Фоншанъ; но иныхъ уже нѣтъ,
другіе странствуютъ далече.
Сади.

МОСКВА.

ВЪ ТИПОГРАФІИ АВГУСТА СЕМЕНА,
при ИМПЕРАТОРСКОЙ Медико-Хирургич. Академіи.

1824.

Title page for A.S. Pushkin's
Bakhchisaraiskii fontan. (No. 337)

One of the earliest of Pushkin's romantic poems, *Bakhchisaraiskii Fontan* was written at the age of 25. This paper-bound copy, a first edition, is from the Kayden home library.

338. Pushkin, Aleksandr S. *Brat'ia razboiniki* [The Robber Brothers]. (Pisano v 1822 godu.) Moskva: V tip. A. Semena, 1827. 15 pp.

An adventure poem with romantic overtones, this work reflects Pushkin's fascination with the popular English authors Bryon and Scott. It is from the Kayden home library.

339. Pushkin, Aleksandr S. *The Captain's Daughter and Other Stories*. Translated from the Russian by Ivy and Tatiana Litvinov with an introduction by Kathryn Feuer. Illustrated by Charles Mozley. Westerham, England: Printed for the members of The Limited Editions Club at the Westerham Press, 1971. xv, 227 pp.; illus. (some col.).

No. 12/1500. Signed by the designer and illustrator, Charles Mozley.

340. Pushkin, Aleksandr S. *Eugene Onegin, a Novel in Verse*. A new translation by Babette Deutsch; edited, with a special introduction by Avrahm Yarmolinsky, illustrated with lithographs by Fritz Eichenberg. New York: The Limited Editions Club, 1943. xvi, 178 pp.; illus.

No. 201/1500. Signed by Fritz Eichenberg.

341. Pushkin, Aleksandr S. *Eugene Onegin, a Novel in Verse*. Translated by Eugene M. Kayden. Illustrated by V. Kuzmin. Yellow Springs, Ohio: Antioch Press, 1964. xvi, 208 pp.; illus.

342. Pushkin, Aleksandr S. *The Golden Cockerel*. A new English version. Illustrated by Edmund Dulac. New York: Limited Editions Club, 1950. 41, 3 pp.; col. illus.

No. 434/1500. Signed by Edmund Dulac.

343. Pushkin, Aleksandr S. *Das goldene Fischlein; Der König Soltan; Das goldene Hähnchen.* Illustrated G. Sohlicht; Deutsche Übersetzung Ervin Walter. Berlin: O. Diakov, 1923. 69 pp.; col. illus.

344. Pushkin, Aleksandr S. *Kamennyi gost';* s prilozheniem variantov i istorii teksta [The Stone Guest]. Moskva: Gos. izd-vo, 1925. 86 pp.

345. Pushkin, Aleksandr S. *Little Tragedies.* Translated by Eugene M. Kayden. Illustrated by Vladimir Favorsky. First edition. Yellow Springs, Ohio: Antioch Press, 1965. 96 pp.; illus.

346. Pushkin, Aleksandr S. *Skazka o pope i o rabotnike ego Balde* [The Priest and His Servant Balda]. Risunki D.N. Butorina (Palekh). Moskva-Leningrad: Academia, 1937. 12 pp.; col. illus.

347. Pushkin, Aleksandr S. *Skazka o rybake i rybke* [The Fisherman and the Golden Fish]. Risunki V. Konashevicha. Izd. 2. Moskva: Izd-vo detskoi lit-ry TZK VLKSM, 1936. 16 pp.; col. illus.

348. Pushkin, Aleksandr S. *Skazka o rybake i rybke* [The Fisherman and the Golden Fish]. Risunki I.I. Zubkov (Palekh). Podgotovka teksta M.K. Azadovskogo. Moskva-Leningrad: Academia, 1937. 18, 2 pp.; col. illus.

349. Pushkin, Aleksandr S. *Skazka o zolotom petushke* [The Golden Cockerel]. Risunki I.P. Bagurova (Palekh). Moskva-Leningrad: Academia, 1937. 16, 1 pp.; .col. illus.

350. Pushkin, Aleksandr S. *Skazka o zolotom petushke* [The Golden Cockerel]. Risunki A. Kantorova. Moskva: Izd-vo "Sovetskaia Rossiia", 1961. 26 pp.; col. illus.

351. Pushkin, Aleksandr S. *Skazka o tsare Saltane i o syne ego slavnom i moguchem bogatyre kniaze Gvidone Saltanoviche i o prekrasnoi tsarevne Lebedi* [Tsar Saltan, Prince Gvidon and the Swan-Princess]. Risunki I.I. Zubkova (Palekh). Podgotovka teksta M.K. Azadovskogo. Moskva: Academia, 1937. 48 pp.; col. illus.

> Since its first performance in Moscow in November 1900, children have enjoyed "Skazka o tsare Saltane," an opera by Nikolai Rimsky-Korsakov and a musical introduction to Pushkin's 1832 fairy tale.

352. Pushkin, Aleksandr S. *Skazka o tsare Saltane i o syne ego slavnom i moguchem bogatyre kniaze Gvidone Saltanoviche i o prekrasnoi tsarevne Lebedi* [Tsar Saltan, Prince Gvidon and the Swan-Princess]. Risoval M.N. Iakovlev. Leningrad: Khudozhnik RSFSR, 1959. 66 pp.; illus.

> Eugene Kayden considered M.N. Iakovlev (1880–1942) a genius, one of the best of the Pushkin illustrators whose work was exhibited throughout Europe. While Kayden was among the first subscribers for this book, its popularity in the Soviet Union rapidly caused it to be sold out. He ruefully reported having to pay a black market price.

353. Pushkin, Aleksandr S. *Skazki v illiustratsiiakh E. Pashkova* [Fairy Tales]. Leningrad: 1964. Portfolio; 16 col. plates.

354. Pushkin, Aleksandr S. *Tsar' Nikita i Pervaia noch' braka; eroticheskiia poemy. Desiataia zapovied'. Epigrammy* [Tsar Nikita and the Wedding Night; Erotic Poems]. En Vente, Chez tous les principaux libraires, 1889. 124 pp.

> Despite the continuing popularity of Pushkin's poetry after his death in 1837, his more frivolous work was censored in Russia. Eventually the poems were published in France in the original language. This edition includes one of Pushkin's first poetic experiments, *Gavriliada*, a description of student life. From the Kayden home library.

355. Pushkin, Aleksandr S. *Tsygany* [Gypsies]. (Pisano v 1824 godu) Moskva: V tip. A. Semena, 1827. 91 pp.

356. Racine, Jean B. *Ifigeniia, tragediia v piati deistviiakh* [Iphigenia]. Na rossiiskie stikhi svobodno prelozhennaia. Moskva: V vol'noi tip. I. Reshetnikova, 1796. 96 pp.

357. Ralston, William R. *Russian Folk-Tales*. London: Smith, Elder, 1873. xvi, 382 pp.

358. Ransome, Arthur. *The Fool of the World and the Flying Ship.* A Russian tale illustrated by Uri Shulevitz. New York: Farrar, Strauss and Giroux, 1968. Unpaginated.

359. Ransome, Arthur. *Old Peter's Russian Tales.* With illustrations, cover design, and decorations by Dmitri Mitrokhin. New York: Frederick A. Stokes, 1917. viii, 334 pp.; illus. (some col.).

360. *Respublica, Siue Status Regni Poloniae, Litvaniae, Prvssiae, Livoniae, etc. Diuersorum Autorum.* Lvgd, Batavorum: Ex Officina Elzeviriana, 1642. 417 pp.
 Engraved title page and tail-piece.

Riha Collection.
 Thomas Riha, professor of Russian History at the University of Colorado, Boulder, disappeared in March 1969. His personal library was donated to the Loretto Heights College Library in Denver, Colorado. In November 1986, his library was purchased by the University of Colorado Libraries and the entire collection is now housed in the Special Collections Department in Norlin Library.
 Riha's valuable collection consists of more than 800 books, some maps, microfilm, and one box of photocopies, notes, etc. It deals with Russian and Soviet history (in English and Russian) and includes rare books on Russian theater, one of his special interests. The collection is being kept intact as a tribute to Dr. Riha.

361. Roerich, Nikolai K. *Altai Himalaya; a Travel Diary, by Nicholas Roerich.* With twenty reproductions from paintings. New York: Frederick A. Stokes Company, 1929. xix, 407 pp.; illus.

Title page for *Respublica, Siue Status Regni. . . .* (No. 360)

Roethel, Hans Konrad. *See* Kandinsky, Wassily (No. 172).

362. Romm, Michael. *The Ascent of Mount Stalin.* Translated by A. Brown. London: Lawrence & Wishart, 1936. 270 pp.; illus., map.

363. Rovinskii, Dmitrii A. *Podrobnyi slovar' russkikh gravirovannykh portretov* [Detailed Dictionary of Russian Engraved Portraits]. Sanktpeterburg: Tipografiia Imperatorskoi Akademii Nauk, 1889. 2 v.

364. Rozanov, Sergei G. *The Adventures of Misha.* Translated by Ivy Low; drawings by Alexander Mogilevsky. New York: Frederick A. Stokes, 1938. 2, 83 pp.; illus.

365. *Rozmyślania dominikańskie* [Dominican Meditations]. Wydali i opracowali Karol Górski i Władysław Kuraszkiewicz; Zofia Rożanow, opracowanie ikonograficzne; Tadeusz Dobrzeniecki, wstęp komparatystyczny. Wyd. 1. Wrocław: Zakł. Narodowy im. Ossolińskich, [1965—]. v.-. Illus.

    Facsimile edition of an early sixteenth century manuscript in the Carmelite Convent of Cracow. Library has volume 1.

366. *Russkii istoricheskii sbornik* [A Russian Historical Anthology]. T.1–7 1837–44. Moskva. 7 v.

367. Rydel, Lucjan. *Królowa Jadwiga* [Queen Jadwiga]. Poznań: Wydał Karol Kozłowski, 1910. 324 pp.; illus. (some col.).

368. Ryleev, Kondratii F. *Voinarovskii; sochinenie* [Voinarovskii]. Moskva: V tip. S. Selivanskago, 1825. xxiv, 64 pp.

369. Selver, Paul. *Modern Russian Poetry.* Text and Translation by P. Selver. London: K. Paul, Trench, Trubner. New York: E.P. Dutton, 1917. xvi, 65, 1 pp.

370. Sergievskii, Maksim V. *Tsygansko-russkii slovar': okolo 10,000 slov s prilozheniem grammatiki tsyganskogo iazyka* [Gypsy-Russian Dictionary]. New York: Chalidze Publications, 1981. 191 pp.
   Reprint of the 1938 edition published by Gos. izd-vo inostrannykh i natsional'nykh slovarei, Moskva.

371. Shakespeare, William. *Shekspir* [Works]. V perevode i ob'iasnenii A.L. Sokolovskago. S.-Peterburg: Tip. Udelov, 1894–97. 4 v.

372. Shakespeare, William. *Sonety Shekspira* [Shakespeare's Sonnets]. v perevodakh S. Marshaka. Moskva: Sovetskii pisatel', 1949. 196 pp.; illus.

373. Shakhrai, L. *Makkavei; istoricheskii etiud' dlia evreiskago iunoshestva* [Maccabeus; an Historical Study for Jewish Youth]. Odessa: Izd. Ia. Kh. Shermana, 1901. 47 pp.

374. Shaw, Bernard. *The Rationalization of Russia.* Bloomington: Indiana University Press, 1964. 134 pp.

375. Shenshin, Afanasii A. *Polnoe sobranie stikhotvorenii A.A. Feta* [Complete Collected Poems of A.A. Fet]. S vstup. stat'iami N.N. Strakhova i V.V. Nikol'skago. S.-Peterburg: A.F. Marks, 1912. 2 v.; illus.
   Author's literary pseudonym, A.A. Fet, appears at head of title. The principal topics of Fet's poetry are nature, love, and reflective philosophy.

376. Shevchenko, Taras. *"Zapovit" movamy narodiv svitu* ["Testament" in the Languages of the World]. Kyiv: Vyd-vo Akademii nauk Ukr. RSR, 1960. 95 pp.; illus.

   The author, whose *testament* appears here in 43 languages, is the national poet and "father" of modern Ukrainian political thought.

377. Shklovskii, Victor B. *Khod konia; sbornik statei* [Knight's Move]. Moskva-Berlin: Gelikon, 1923. 296 pp.

378. Sichyns'kyi, Volodymyr. *Taras Shevchenko.* L'viv: N.P., 1938. 38 pp.; illus.

379. Sitwell, Edith. *The Collected Poems.* Frontispiece by Pavel Tcheletchew. London: Duckworth, Boston: Houghton Mifflin, 1930. x, 278 pp.; illus.

   No. 257/320. Signed by the author.

380. Skachinskii, Aleksandr. *Slovar' blatnogo zhargona v SSSR* [Dictionary of Prison Slang in the USSR]. N'iu-Iork: Silver Age Press. 1982. 246 pp.

381. *Skazki* [Fairy Tales]. Risunki I.Ia. Bilibina. S.-Peterburg: Izdanie Ekspeditsii zagotovleniia gosudarstvennykh bumag, 1901–1903. 8 v. in l; col. illus.

382. Skobtsova, Evgeniia I. *Dostoevskii i sovremennost'* [Dostoevskii and Modernity]. Paris: YMCA Press, 1929. 73 pp.

383. Sládkovič, Andrej. *Marína.* Vyd. v SVKL 4. Bratislava: Slovenské vydavateľstvo krásnej literatúry, 1965. 319 pp.; illus.

384. Slesser, Malcolm. *Red Peak.* A personal account of the British-Soviet Pamir Expedition, 1962. London: Hodder and Stoughton, 1964. 256 pp.; illus. (some col.), maps.

385. Slesser, Malcolm. *Red Peak.* A personal account of the British-Soviet Pamir Expedition, 1962. New York: Coward-McCann., 1964. 256 pp.; illus. (some col.), maps.

386. *Slovo o pokhode Igorevom, Igoria syna Sviatoslava, vnuka Olegova* [The Igor Tale]. Podgotovka teksta, perevod i posleslovie D.S. Likhacheva. Khudozhnik Vladimir Semenov. Leningrad: Khudozhnik RSFSR, 1971. 111 pp.; col. illus.

    The greatest and most puzzling work of literature of Kievan Rus'.

387. *Slovo o polku Igoria Sviatoslavicha, udiel'nago kniazia Novgorod - Sieverskago* [The Igor Tale]. Vnov' perelozhennoe Iakovom Pozharskim s prisovokupleniem primiechanii. Sanktpeterburg: V tip. Departamenta narodnago prosveshcheniia, 1819. 88, 35 pp.

    In a diced russia leather binding with modern slipcase. Bound with the printed work are 35 pages of holographic explanatory notes by Nikolai T. Beliaev.

388. *Slovo o polku Igorevie: tekst pamiatnika, perevody, istoriia pokhoda Igoria, kriticheskii obzor* [The Igor Tale]. Klassnoe izd. Pod red. V. Nikol'skago. S.-Peterburg: Izd. Akts. o-va tip. Diela, 1911. 81 pp.

Slovo o polku Igorevie. *See also* Favorskii, Vladimir A.

389. Smal-Stocki, Roman. *Znachinnia ukrains'kykh prykmentnykiv* [Ukrainian Adjectives]. Varshava: Nakladnia L. Idzikovs'koho, 1926. 85 pp.

390. Soboleska, Mme. *Les cinq nièces de l'oncle Barbe-Bleue, par Jacques Lermont.* Paris: Charavay, Mantoux, Martin, [1892?]. 227 pp.; illus.

    Author's presentation copy to Mary Rippon, first woman professor at the University of Colorado.

391. Sobolev, Nikolai N. *Russkaia narodnaia rez'ba po derevu* [Russian Wood Carvings]. Moskva: Academia, 1934. 476 pp.; illus.

392. *Sobranie russkikh vorovskikh slovarei* [Collection of Russian Thieves' Slang Dictionaries]. Sostavlenie i primechaniia Vladimira Kozlovskogo. New York: Chalidze Pub., 1983. 4 v.
    Reprint of works originally published 1859 to 1971.

393. Soiuz vyzvolennia Ukrainy [Society for the Liberation of Ukraine]. *Samostiina Ukraina* [Independent Ukraine]. R.U.P. Vetsliar, 1917. 43 pp.

394. Sokolov, Nikolai M. *Lirika Ia.P. Polonskago; kriticheskii etiud* [The Lyric Poetry of Ia. P. Polonskii]. S.-Peterburg: Izdanie P.P. Soikina, 1898. 99 pp.

Sologub, Vladimir. *See* Teternikov, Fedor K.

395. *Souvenir, Serge de Diaghileff's Ballet Russe.* New York: Metropolitan Ballet Co., Inc. [1916]. Unpaginated; illus. (some col.).
    Quarter-bound by noted Denver bookbinder, Edward McLean, in morocco with cloth box.

396. *Sovremennaia literatura* [Contemporary Literature]. Sbornik statei. Leningrad: Mysl', 1925. 182 pp.

397. Soria, Georges. *Trotskyism in the Service of Franco; Facts and Documents on the Activities of the P.O.U.M.* London: Lawrence and Wishart, 1938. 48 pp.

398. Stafford, Jean. *Zły charakter.* Warszawa: Państwowy Instytut Wydawniczy, 1978. 309 pp.
    Selections from *The Collected Stories of Jean Stafford.*

399. Stein, Gertrude. *On our Way, by Gertrude Stein & Alice B. Toklas.* New York: Printed by Schuster, 1959. 11 pp.

    Correspondence to Allen Tanner and Pavel Tchelitcheff in a limited edition. This is No. 51/100.

400. Steinbeck, John. *A Russian Journal.* With photographs by Robert Capa. New York: Viking Press, 1948. 220 pp.; illus.

401. Stemann, Ingeborg. *Russike bønder fortaeller.* København: Martin, 1932. 126 pp.

402. Štitný, Tomáš. *Knižky o hospodářovi, a hospodyni a o čeledi* [Rural Etiquette]. K tisku upravil a poznámkami opatřil V. Foch. Praha: 1929. 141 pp.; illus.

403. Strahlenberg, Philip. *An Historico-Geographical Description of the North and Eastern Parts of Europe and Asia; but more particularly of Russia, Siberia, and Great Tartary; Both in their Ancient and Modern State: Together With An entire New Polyglot-Table of the Dialects of 32 Tartarian Nations. . . .* Written Originally in High German. Now faithfully translated into English. London: Printed for J. Brotherton *et al.* 1738. ix, 463 pp.; illus., maps.

404. Struve, Gleb. *Ital'ianskie obrazy i motivy v poezii Osipa Mandel'shtama* [Italian Images and Motifs in the Poetry of Osip Mandel'shtam]. Estratto da: "Studi in onore di Ettore Lo Gatto e Giovanni Maver." Firenze: Sansoni, 1962. 13 pp.

    Reprint sent "To Dr. Eugene M. Kayden with best wishes for Christmas and New Year from Gleb Struve, Dec. 1962."

405. *Tales of Rus-land.* With illustrations by Ivan A. Bilibin. [n.p.]. [n.d.]. 5 pp.; col. illus.

    Incomplete. Library has *The Epic Song of Knight Volhga* only.

Tcherepov, Ivan A. *See* Cherepov, Ivan A.

406. Teternikov, Fedor K. *Sobranie sochinenenii* [Collected works].
SPB: Spring, 1913. v.-. Illus.

Library has volumes 1, 5, 9, 13, 17.

Author's literary pseudonym, Vladimir Sologub, appears at the
head of title. Symbolist poet, novelist, short story writer, and dramatist,
his idealistic philosophy and fantasies run counter to Socialist realism.

407. Tetmajer, Kazimierz. *Kazimierz Przerwa-Tetmajer.* Warszawa:
Czytelnik, 1966. 142 pp.

The most characteristic and popular poet of the early "Young Poland"
era.

408. *Théâtre Serge de Diaghilew: Les biches. . . .* Paris: Éditions
des Quatre Chemins, 1924. 2 v. in 1; illus. (some col.), music.

Originating on the occasion of Sergei Diaghilev's production of *Les
Biches* (January 6, 1924 in the Théatre de Monte-Carlo), this book
is a fine document of the Russian influence on the artistic climate
in France between the wars. This copy, number 29 of the first 60
copies, is on Van Gelder paper, bound by Gruel in full grey morocco,
with morocco inlays in yellow, purple, and gold. Inner decorations
consist of purple and gold morocco inlays and red moirée doublures.

Music for the ballet was composed by François Poulenc; the costumes
and settings were by Marie Laurencin. Darius Milhaud contributed
an article on Poulenc, including the reproduction of a page from
the composer's score. Jean Cocteau contributed articles on the ballet
and its performance as well as one on Marie Laurencin, the artist
whose drawings and watercolors for the ballet and its costumes are
finely reproduced. A drawing by Cocteau and photographs by Man
Ray and Georges Détaille round out this elegant production enclosed
in its attractive slipcase.

409. Tikhonravov, Nikolai S. *Pamiatniki otrechennoi russkoi literatury* [Monuments of Alienated Russian Literature]. Sanktpeterburg:
V Tip. t-va "Obshchestvennaia Pol'za", 1863. 2 v.; illus.

Title page illustration for "Les Biches" by M. Laurencin
from *Théâtre Serge de Diaghilew.* . . . (No. 408)

410. Tille, V. *Little Tom.* Illustrated by O. Štáfl. Prague: B. Kočí, 1922. 134 pp.; illus. (some col.).

411. Tiutchev, Fedor I. *Polnoe sobranie sochinenii* [Collected Works]. Pod red. P.V. Bykova. S.-Peterburg: Izd. T-va A.F. Marksa, 1913. 468 pp.

412. Tiutchev, Fedor I. *Stikhotvoreniia* [Poems]. Sanktpeterburg: V tip. E. Pratsa, 1854. 139 pp.

> In a letter to the University of Colorado librarian, dated June 30, 1974, Eugene Kayden wrote, "Of Tyutchev, you have the first edition edited by Turgenev (think of it!), a slender booklet, dated 1854." He recommended that the title page be reproduced for a book on Tiutchev.

413. Tolstoi, Aleksei N. *Nikita's Childhood.* Moscow: Foreign Languages Publishing House, n.d. 136 pp.; illus.

414. Tolstoi, Aleksei N. *Tsarevna-liagushka;* [The Frog-Princess]. Russkaia narodnaia skazka v obrabotke A.N. Tolstogo. Risunki I. Bilibina. Moskva: Sovetskaia Rossiia, 1961. 16 pp.; col. illus.

415. Tolstoi, Il'ia L. One-page holograph letter to Mrs. Heald, Oct. 30, 1928.

> Headed "211 W. 101 Street." Signed "Count Ilya Tolstoy," the writer regrets, in English, that he will no longer be speaking in New York as he is going "to the West." He is happy that Mrs. Heald is interested in his father's philosophy because it "is the religion of the future."

416. Tolstoi, Il'ia L. Two-page holographic letter to Mrs. Heald, Jan. 13, 1931.

> Headed "35 St. Nicholas Terrace (128 St) apt. 61., phone: Cath. 1600." Signed "Count Ilya Tolstoy," the writer expresses in English his happiness "to meet people who understand and are able to appreciate the great message of my father."

417. Tolstoi, Lev N. *Anna Karenina*. Translated by Constance Garnett, edited by Bernard Guilbert Guerney and Gustavus Spett with an introduction by Anatole Lunacharsky and with wood-engravings by Nikolas Piskariov. Moscow: State Publishing House for Fiction and Poetry, 1933. 2 v.; col. illus.

    Printed for the Limited Editions Club. No. 1250/1500. Signed by N. Piskariov.

418. Tolstoi, Lev N. *Anna Karenina*. Translated by Constance Garnett. The text edited and revised by Gustavus Spett and the translation revised by Bernard Guilbert Guerney. Illustrated with lithographs by Barnett Freedman. Cambridge, England: Cambridge University Press, 1951. 2 v.; col. illus.

    Printed for the Limited Editions Club. No. 434/1500. Signed by B. Freedman.

419. Tolstoi, Lev N. Four-page holographic letter in English, signed, to Ernest Crosby, July 11, 1898.

    Discussion of the plight of the Doukhobors wishing to emigrate from Russia, as well as the cost of passage and settlement in Texas.

420. Tolstoi, Lev N. *Bogu ili mammonie?* [God or Mammon?]. Moskva: Tip. T-va. I.D. Sytina, 1896. 23 pp.

421. Tolstoi, Lev N. *Malysham* [For Kids]. Risunki A. Pakhomova. Leningrad: Gos. izd-vo detskoi lit-ry, 1960. 39 pp.; illus.

422. Tolstoi, Lev N. *Resurrection; a novel in three parts by Leo Tolstoy*. Translated by Leo Wiener, revised and edited for this edition by F.D. Reeve. With an introduction by Ernest J. Simmons and illustrated with wood-engravings by Fritz Eichenberg. New York: Limited Editions Club, 1963. xvii, 403 pp.; illus.

    No. 12/1500. Signed by Fritz Eichenberg.

423. Tolstoi, Lev N. *War and Peace.* Translated by Louise and Aylmer Maude, with a special introduction for this edition by Aylmer Maude. Illustrated with lithographs and drawings by Barnett Freedman. Glasgow: University Press, 1938. 6 v.; illus. (some col.).

> Printed for the Limited Editions Club. No. 1119/1500. Signed by B. Freedman.

424. Tolstoi, Nadine. Two-page holographic letter, signed, to Mrs. Heald [n.d.].

> Written on stationery with letterhead in gold showing Tolstoy crest over "Tolstoy's Hill Southbury, Conn." Countess Tolstoy regrets that she and the Count cannot accept the "kind invitation."

425. *Trebnyk* [Prayer Book]. Kiev: Kievo-Pecherskaia Lavra, 1864. 384 pp.

> Text in Church Slavonic.

426. Trotskii, Lev. *The Permanent Revolution.* Translated by Max Shachtman. New York: Pioneer Publishers, 1931. xlviii, 157 pp.

427. Turgenev, Ivan S. *Dream Tales and Prose Poems.* Translated by Constance Garnett. New York: Macmillan, 1897. 323 pp.

428. Turgenev, Ivan S. *Fathers and Sons.* Translated by Constance Garnett, with preface by John T. Winterich, illustrated with wood engravings by Fritz Eichenberg. New York: The Spiral Press, 1951. viii, 215 pp.; illus.

> Printed for the Limited Editions Club. No. 434/1500. Signed by Fritz Eichenberg.

429. Turgenev, Ivan S. *The Torrents of Spring.* Translated by David Magarshack, illustrated by Faith Jaques. London: Folio Society, 1967. 167 pp.; illus.

430. Turner, Samuel. *Siberia, a Record of Travel, Climbing, and Exploration.* Introduction by Baron Heyking. Illustrated with photographs by the author. London: T. Fisher Unwin, 1905. 440 pp.; illus.

431. Turner, Samuel. *Siberia, a Record of Travel, Climbing, and Exploration.* London: T. Fisher Unwin, 1911. Second edition. 320 pp.; illus.

432. Ullman, James R. *Człowiek Everestu* [Man of Everest]. Translated by Maria Skroczyńska. Warszawa: Iskry, 1957. 335 pp.; illus.

433. Ullman, James R. *Muž z Everestu; Tensingova autobiografie* [The Man from Everest]. Translated by Melanie Rybarova. Praha: Sportovní a Turistické Nakladatelství, 1959. 224 pp.; illus.

434. *Ustava Československé socialistické republiky* [Czechoslovak Republic. Constitution]. Praha: Mladá fronta, 1960. 141 pp.

435. Ustimovich, Petr M. *Mikhailovskoe, Trigorskoe i mogila Pushkina* [Mikhailovskoe, Trigorskoe and Pushkin's Grave]. S illiustratsiiami po fotografiiam V.M. Fedorova i bibliografiei. Leningrad: Izd-vo Akademii nauk SSSR, 1927. 51 pp.; illus., map.

> Described by Eugene Kayden as a very rare item, the University of Colorado Libraries has two copies.

436. *V.O. Kliuchevskii; Kharakterisitiki i vospominaniia* [Kliuchevskii; Character Descriptions and Memoirs]. Moskva: Nauchnoe slovo, 1912. 217 pp.

437. Varshavskii, L. P. *Russkaia karikatura 40-50-kh gg. XIX v.* [Russian Cartoons from the First Half of the Nineteenth Century]. Khudozhnik knigi A.I. Iglin. Moskva: OGIZ-IZOGIZ, 1937. 143 pp.; illus.

438. *Vienok na mogilu Sergieia Andreevicha Muromtseva* [A Wreath for the Grave of Sergei Muromtsev]. Moskva: 1910. 263 pp.; illus.

"Pamiati Sergieia Adndreevicha Muromtseva, druz'ia i pochitateli. Pod red. V.P. Obninskago."

439. Vigne, Godfrey T. *A Personal Narrative of a Visit to Ghuzni, Kabul, and Afghanistan, and of a Residence at the Court of Dost Mohamed: With Notices of Runjit Sing, Khiva, and the Russian Expedition.* London: Whittaker, 1840. 479 pp.; illus. (some col.).

440. Vinson, Pauline. *Hilltop Russians in San Francisco.* Pictures by Pauline Vinson, text by William Saroyan. Palo Alto: J. Delkin, 1941. Unpaginated; illus.

"Five hundred copies printed at The Grabhorn Press in December MCMXLI."

441. Vishniac, Roman. *Polish Jews, a Pictorial Record.* With an introductory essay by Abraham Joshua Heschel. New York: Schocken Books, 1965. 16 pp.; illus.

Author's initialed presentation copy.

442. Voloshin, Maksimilian A. *Demony glukhonemye* [Deaf and Dumb Demons]. 2 izd. Berlin: Kn-vo pisatelei v Berline, 1923. 72 pp.

443. Voltaire, François M. *The History of The Russian Empire Under Peter the Great.* Glasgow: Printed for Robert Urie, 1764. xiii, 324 pp.

444. Vorivoda, Ivan P. *Sbornik zhargonnykh slov i vyrazhenii, upotrebliaemykh v ustnoi rechi prestupnym elementom* [A Collection of Slang With Expressions Used by Criminals in Spoken Russian]. Alma-Ata: Tip. MVD KazSSR, 1971. 102 pp.

Reprint.

445. Vrusianin, V. V. *Ukazatel' knig i statei o Gosudarstvennoi Dume* [Index of Books and Articles on Parliament]. Moskva: Knigoizdatel'stvo "Nauka", 1913. 92 pp.

446. Vzdornov, Gerol'd I. *Issledovanie o Kievskoi Psaltiri* [Research on the Kievan Psalter]. Moskva: Iskusstvo, 1978. 171 pp.; illus.
> Issued in a slipcase with: Bible. O.T. Church Slavic. Kievskaia Psaltir'. (*See* No. 34.)

447. Wheeler, Post. *Russian Wonder Tales.* Containing Twelve of the famous Bilibin illustrations in color. New York: Century, 1912. xix, 323 pp.

448. Whitney, Thomas P. *The Story of Prince Ivan, the Firebird, and the Gray Wolf.* Illustrated by Nonny Hogrogian. New York: Charles Scribner, 1968. Unpaginated.

449. Wierzyński, Kazimierz *Selected Poems.* Edited by Clark Mills and Ludwik Krzyzanowski. Introduction by Donald Davie. New York: Voyages Press, 1959. 45 pp.; illus.
> Living in exile in America after 1939, Wierzynski's neo-classicism defined his life attitudes as well as his verse forms.

450. Winawer, Bruno. *The Book of Job: a Satirical Comedy.* Translated by Josef Conrad. London and Toronto: J.M. Dent, 1931. xvi, 143 pp.

451. Wyspiański, Stanisław. *Dzieła malarskie* [Artistic Works]. Tekst napisali: Stanisław Przybyszewski i Tadeusz Zuk-Skarszewski. Warszawa: Inst. Wyd. "Bibljoteka Polska", 1925. 131 pp.; illus. (some col.).

Yevtushenko, Yevgeny A. *See* Evtushenko, Evgenii A.

Self portrait by S. Wyspiański
from *Dzieła malarskie*. (No. 451)

452. Zakharchenko, M. *Kiev teper' i prezhde* [Kiev, Now and Then]. Izdal S.V. Kul'zhenko. Risunki i klishe sobstvennost' izdatelia. Kiev: S.V. Kul'zhenko, 1888. 290 pp.; illus., plans.

453. *Zoria Halytska* [Galician Star]. Ch. 7 Dnia 27 chervtsia, 1848. L'vov: Zaruchaiushchii vyd. Ia. Paventskyi. Typom Institutu Stavropigiian'skogo.

Official newspaper of the Supreme Ruthenian Council in L'viv.

ADDENDA

454. Mandel, Dorothy I. *Russian Suite*: Portfolio containing ten woodcut prints. Illustrations commissioned for Eugene M. Kayden's last translations: *Russian Poems* and *Three Stories*. Boulder, Colorado: Colorado Quarterly, 1979.

No. 1/60 with all prints signed by the artist.

455. Nomys, Matvii. *Ukrains'ki prykazky, prysliv'ia i take inshe* [Ukrainian Proverbs, Adages and Other Sayings]. Saut-Bavnd-Bruk, N.Dzh.: Vyd. fond vladyky Mstyslava, Oselia sv. Andriia Pervozvannoho, 1985. 2 v.; illus. V. 1: Ukrains'ki prykazky. V. 2: Folkl'ornyi zbirnyk Matviia Nomysa.

A reprint originally published in S.-Petersburg, 1864.

456. *Skazanie o Borise i Glebe* [The Legend of Boris and Gleb]. Avtory L.A. Dmitriev [*et al.*] Khud. B.P. Zhuravskii. Faksim. vosproizvedenie zhitiinykh povestei iz Sil'vestrovskogo sbornika (2-ia pol. XIX v.) Moskva: Kniga, 1985. 2 v.; illus. v. 1: Nauchno-spravochnyi aparat izd. v. 2: Faksim. izd.

457. Vovchok, Marko. *Chary* [Charms]. Peterburg: V drukarni P.A. Kulisha, 1860. 17 pp.

INDICES

Numbers refer to the catalog listing and not to the page number.